LIVING LANGUAGE®

ITALIAN
COURSEBOOK

REVISED & UPDATED

THE LIVING LANGUAGE® SERIES

**Living Language® Basic Complete
 Courses Revised & Updated**
Spanish   *Japanese*
French   *Russian*
German   *Italian*
Portuguese
Inglés/English for Spanish Speakers

**Living Language® 2000+
 Essential Verbs**
French   *Spanish*

**Living Language® Intermediate
 Skill Builder Courses**
German Verbs   *Italian Verbs*

**Living Language® Advanced Courses,
 Revised & Updated**
Advanced Spanish   *Advanced French*

Living Language® Ultimate™
 (formerly **All the Way™**)
Spanish   *Advanced Spanish*
French   *Advanced French*
German   *Advanced German*
Italian   *Advanced Italian*
Russian   *Advanced Russian*
Japanese   *Advanced Japanese*
Inglés/English for Spanish Speakers
*Advanced Inglés/English for Spanish
 Speakers*
Mandarin Chinese
Portuguese

Living Language® Without the Fuss
French   *Italian*   *Spanish*

**Living Language® English
 for New Americans**
Everyday Life
Health & Safety
Work & School

Living Language® All-Audio™
Spanish   *French*   *Italian*   *German*

**Living Language® American English
 Pronunciation Program**

Fodor's Languages for Travelers
Spanish   *French*   *Italian*   *German*

**Living Language® Parent/Child
 Activity Kits**
Learn French Together
Learn Italian Together
Learn Spanish Together
Learn French Together: For the Car
Learn Italian Together: For the Car
Learn Spanish Together: For the Car

**Living Language® Business
 Companion**
Chinese   *French*
German   *Japanese*
Spanish

If you're traveling, we recommend
Fodor's guides

Available in bookstores everywhere

Visit our Web site at: **www.livinglanguage.com** for more informaiton

Living Language® publications are available at special discounts for bulk
purchases for sales promotions or premiums, as well as for fund-raising or
educational use. Special editions can be created in large quantities for
special needs. For more information, write to Special Sales Manager,
Living Language, 1745 Broadway, New York, NY 10019.

ITALIAN
COURSEBOOK

REVISED & UPDATED

REVISED BY LORRAINE-MARIE GATTO

Based on the original

by Genevieve A. Martin

and Mario Ciatti

◆

Based on the method devised

by Ralph Weiman, Former Chief of

Language Section, U.S. War Department

LIVING LANGUAGE®
A Random House Company

CONTENTS

v

INTRODUCTION

Living Language® Italian makes it easy to learn how to speak, read, and write Italian. This course is a thoroughly revised and updated version of *Living Italian: The Complete Living Language Course®*. The same highly effective method of language instruction is still used, but the content has been updated to reflect modern usage, and the format has been clarified. In this course, the basic elements of the language have been carefully selected and condensed into forty short lessons. If you can study about thirty minutes a day, you can master this course and learn to speak Italian in a few weeks.

This *Living Language® Italian Coursebook* provides English translations and brief explanations for each lesson. The first five lessons cover pronunciation, laying the foundation for learning the vocabulary, phrases, and grammar that are explained in the later chapters. If you already know a little Italian, you can use the book as a phrase book and reference. In addition to the forty lessons, there is a Summary of Italian Grammar, plus verb conjugations, and a section on letter writing.

Also included in the course package is the *Living Language® Italian Dictionary*. It contains more than 15,000 entries, with many of the definitions illustrated by phrases and idiomatic expressions. More than 1,000 of the most essential words are capitalized to make them easy to find. You can increase your vocabulary and range of expression just by browsing through the dictionary.

Practice your Italian as much as possible, even if you can't manage a trip abroad. Watching Italian movies, reading Italian magazines, eating at Italian restaurants, and talking with Italian-speaking friends are enjoyable ways to help you reinforce what you have learned with *Living Language®️ Italian*. Now, let's begin.

The following instructions will tell you what to do. *Buona fortuna!* Good luck!

COURSE MATERIAL

1. Two 90-minute cassettes or three 60-minute compact discs.

2. *Living Language®️ Italian Coursebook.* This book is designed for use with the recorded lessons, but it may also be used alone as a reference. It contains the following sections:

   Basic Italian in 40 Lessons
   Summary of Italian Grammar
   Verb Conjugations
   Letter Writing

3. *Living Language®️ Italian Dictionary:* The Italian/ English–English/Italian dictionary contains more than 15,000 entries. Phrases and idiomatic expressions illustrate many of the definitions. More than 1,000 of the most essential words are capitalized.

INSTRUCTIONS

1. Look at page 1. The words in **boldface** type are the ones you will hear on the recording.

2. Now read Lesson 1 all the way through. Note the points to listen for when you play the recording. The first word you will hear is **Alfredo.**

3. Start the recording, listen carefully, and say the words aloud in the pauses provided. Go through the lesson once and don't worry if you can't pronounce everything correctly the first time around. Try it again and keep repeating the lesson until you are comfortable with it. The more often you listen and repeat, the longer you will remember the material.

4. Now go on to the next lesson. If you take a break between lessons, it's always good to review the previous lesson before starting a new one.

5. In the manual, there are two kinds of quizzes. With matching quizzes, you must select the English translation of the Italian sentence. The other type requires you to fill in the blanks with the correct Italian word chosen from the three given directly below the sentence. If you make any mistakes, begin again and reread the section.

6. Even after you have finished the forty lessons and achieved a perfect score on the Final Quiz, keep practicing your Italian by listening to the recordings and conversing with Italian-speaking friends. For further study, try *Living Language® Ultimate Italian, All-Audio Italian,* and Fodor's *Italian for Travelers.*

LIVING LANGUAGE®

ITALIAN
COURSEBOOK

REVISED & UPDATED

LESSON 1

A. SOUNDS OF THE ITALIAN LANGUAGE

Many Italian sounds are similar to the English. Listen to and repeat the following Italian names, and notice which sounds are similar and which are different:

Alfredo	Alfred	**Luigi**	Louis
Antonio	Anthony	**Luisa**	Louise
Carlo	Charles	**Maria**	Mary
Caterina	Katherine	**Michele**	Michael
Enrico	Henry	**Paolo**	Paul
Elisabetta	Elizabeth	**Peppino**	Joe
Emanuele	Emanuel	**Pietro**	Peter
Ferdinando	Ferdinand	**Raffaele**	Raphael
Francesco	Francis	**Raimondo**	Raymond
Giovanni	John	**Riccardo**	Richard
Giorgio	George	**Roberto**	Robert
Giulia	Julia	**Rosa**	Rose
Giuseppe	Joseph	**Vincenzo**	Vincent
Isabella	Isabel	**Violetta**	Violet

NOTE:

1. That each vowel is pronounced clearly and crisply.

2. That a single consonant is pronounced with the following vowel.

3. That some vowels bear an accent mark, which sometimes shows the accentuated syllable:

la città   the city

but sometimes merely serves to distinguish words:

e   and   è   is

4. When the accent is on the letter *e,* it gives a more open pronunciation:

caffè   coffee

5. The apostrophe (') is used to mark elision, the omission of a vowel. For example, when the word *dove* (where) is combined with *è* (is), the *e* in *dove* is dropped: *Dov'è?* Where is?

Now listen to some geographical names:

Bari	**Napoli**
Brindisi	**Ravenna**
Genova	**Sardegna**
Legnano	**Sicilia**
Livorno	**Taranto**
Messina	**Urbino**
Milano	**Venezia**

Now the names of some countries:

Argentina	**Inghilterra**
Belgio	**Messico**
Cina	**Norvegia**
Spagna	**Giappone**
Stati Uniti	**Portogallo**
India	**Egitto**
Francia	**Venezuela**
Germania	**Russia**

B. COGNATES: WORDS SIMILAR IN ENGLISH AND ITALIAN

Now listen to and repeat the following cognates (words that are similar in English and Italian). Notice how Italian spelling and pronunciation differ from English:

azione	action	**certo**	certain
agente	agent	**chitarra**	guitar
attenzione	attention	**differente**	different
caso	case	**difficile**	difficult
centro	center	**esempio**	example

festa	feast	**ristorante**	restaurant
importante	important	**simile**	similar
interessante	interesting	**té**	tea
nazione	nation	**teatro**	theater
necessario	necessary	**telefono**	telephone
possibile	possible	**treno**	train
radio	radio	**visita**	visit

LESSON 2

A. THE ITALIAN ALPHABET

LETTER	NAME	LETTER	NAME	LETTER	NAME
a	*a*	h	*acca*	q	*qu*
b	*bi*	i	*i*	r	*erre*
c	*ci*	l	*elle*	s	*esse*
d	*di*	m	*emme*	t	*ti*
e	*e*	n	*enne*	u	*u*
f	*effe*	o	*o*	v	*vu*
g	*gi*	p	*pi*	z	*zeta*

B. PRONUNCIATION PRACTICE WITH COGNATES

The following groups of cognates will give you some additional practice in Italian pronunciation and spelling:

attore	actor	**generoso**	generous
animale	animal	**generale**	general
capitale	capital	**umore**	humor
centrale	central	**locale**	local
cereale	cereal	**materiale**	material
cioccolato	chocolate	**originale**	original
colore	color	**personale**	personal
dottore	doctor	**probabile**	probable
familiare	familiar	**regolare**	regular

simile	similar	**totale**	total
semplice	simple	**usuale**	usual

LESSON 3

A. Vowels

1. *a* is like *ah*, or the *a* in *father*:

a	to, at	**lago**	lake
amico	friend *(masc.)*	**pane**	bread
la	the *(fem.sing.)*[1]	**parlare**	to speak

2. *e* is like the *e* in *cent*:

era	was	**treno**	train
essere	to be	**tre**	three
pera	pear	**estate**	summer
padre	father	**se**	if
carne	meat		

e in the middle of a word may have two different sounds when stressed:

OPEN SOUND		CLOSED SOUND	
me	me	**verde**	green
e	and	**venti**	twenty
tre	three	**tema**	fear

---

[1] *fem.sing.* stands for *feminine singular*. In Italian, nouns are either masculine or feminine, and the words that modify them agree in gender and number (singular or pural).

3. *i* is like the *i* in *police, machine, marine*, but not drawled:

misura	measure	**oggi**	today
sì	yes	**piccolo**	small *(masc.sing.)*
amica	friend *(fem.)*	**figlio**	son

4. *o* is like the *o* in *no*, but not drawled:

no	no	**con**	with
poi	then	**otto**	eight
ora	hour	**come**	how
sono	am, are	**forma**	form
corpo	body	**voce**	voice

5. *u* is like the *u* in *rule*, but not drawled:

uno	one *(masc.)*	**tu**	you *(familiar)*[1]
una	one *(fem.)*	**ultimo**	last

6. Notice that each vowel is clearly pronounced, and that Italian vowels tend to be shorter and crisper than English vowels:

Europa	Europe	**poesia**	poem
leggere	to read	**creare**	to create
dov'è	where is	**mio**	my
io sono	I am	**paese**	country
idea	idea		

---

[1] Italian distinguishes between familiar and polite forms of "you." The *tu* form is reserved for children, close friends, relatives, and pets. Use the *Lei* form, which is more polite, when addressing people you have just met, as well as with professionals and others you wish to show respect for.

B. DIPHTHONGS: DOUBLE VOWEL COMBINATIONS

1. *ai:*

guai	troubles		

2. *au:*

aula	room	**autunno**	autumn

3. *ei:*

sei	six	**dei**	of the

4. *eu:*

Europa	Europe	**neutro**	neutral

5. *ia:*

Italia	Italy	**patria**	homeland

6. *ie:*

piede	foot	**tieni**	(you) keep

7. *io:*

stazione	station	**piove**	it is raining

8. *iu:*

fiume	river	**piuma**	feather

9. *oi:*

poi	then	**noi**	we

10. *ua:*

quale	what	**quattro**	four

11. *ue:*

questo	this	**quello**	that

12. *ui:*

buio	darkness	**lui**	him

13. *uo:*

buono	good	**tuo**	your (*familiar*)

C. Triphthongs: Triple Vowel Combinations

1. *iei* (pronounce: yeh-ee):

miei   my

2. *iuo* (pronounce: you-oh):

figliuolo   son

3. *uoi* (pronounce: woe-ee):

tuoi   your *(familiar)*

LESSON 4

A. Consonants

1. *b* is pronounced like the English *b* in *boat*:

bottiglia   bottle

2. *c* has two different sounds:

before *a, o, u*, it is equivalent to the English *k* in *bake:*

caso   case

before *e* or *i* it is equivalent to the English *ch* in *church*:

celibe   bachelor

3. *d* is like the English *d* in *dark:*

data   date

4. *f* is equivalent to the English *f:*

forza   force

5. *g* has two different sounds: before *a, o, u*, it is equivalent to the English *g* in *go:*

guida   guide

before *e* or *i*, it is equivalent to the English *g* in *general*:

generoso   generous

6. *h* is not pronounced. It is found only in exclamations:

Ah!   Ah!

in certain forms of the verb *to have*:

io ho   I have

or in words of foreign origin:

hotel   hotel

7. *l, m, n, p* are equivalent to the corresponding letters in English:

libertà	liberty	**notte**	night
memoria	memory	**prova**	proof

8. *q* is used only in combination with *u* and is pronounced like the English *qu* in *quality*.

quarto   quarter

9. *r* is rolled, similar to Spanish pronunciation:

regione   region

10. *s* has two different sounds:

at the beginning of a word, when used double, or when followed by another consonant it is equivalent to the *s* in *song*:

sale	salt	**fresco**	cool
rosso	red		

when occurring between two vowels it sounds like a *z*:

causa	cause	**poesia**	poetry
esilio	exile		

11. *t, v* are equivalent to the corresponding letters in English:

tono	tone	**vacanza**	vacation

12. *z* has two different sounds:

harsh, as in the English combination *ts*. This sound generally occurs in the group *-zione*.

azione	action	**addizione** addition
nazione	nation	

soft, as in the English combination *ds*. This sound occurs mostly in technical and classical words derived from Greek.

zona	zone	**zebra**	zebra

B. SPECIAL ITALIAN SOUNDS

Pay special attention to the following sounds, which do not have exact English equivalents:

1. *cc* when followed by *i* or *e* is pronounced like the English *ch* in *chair:*

cacciatore	hunter	**faccia**	face

2. *ch* before *e* and *i* is pronounced like the English *k* in *key:*

chitarra	guitar	**chiodo**	nail

3. *gh* before *e* and *i* is pronounced like the English *g* in *gate:*

ghiaccio	ice	**ghetto**	ghetto

4. *gli* is always pronounced as one letter; the closest English approximation would be the combination *lli*, as in *million:*

figlia	daughter	**paglia**	straw
foglia	leaf	**giglio**	lily

5. *gn* is always pronounced as one letter, somewhat like the English *ni* in *onion,* or *ny* in *canyon:*

segno	sign	**Spagna**	Spain
montagna	mountain	**lavagna**	blackboard

6. *sc* before *e* and *i* is pronounced like the English *sh* in *shoe:*

scendere	(to) climb	**sciroppo**	syrup
scimmia	monkey	**scivolare**	(to) slip

7. *sc* before *a, o,* and *u* is pronounced like the English *sk* in *sky:*

scuola	school	**Scozia**	Scotland
scarpa	shoe	**scoiattolo**	squirrel

C. MORE ITALIAN-ENGLISH COGNATES

Building up an Italian vocabulary is fairly easy since a great number of words are similar in English and Italian. Some words are spelled exactly the same (though they may differ considerably in pronunciation):

ITALIAN	ENGLISH	ITALIAN	ENGLISH
antenna	antenna	**zoo**	zoo
area	area	**idea**	idea
auto	auto	**opera**	opera
radio	radio	**cinema**	cinema

There are many Italian words that you will have no difficulty in recognizing despite minor differences. Some of these differences are:

1. The Italian words add *e*.

annuale	annual	**origine**	origin
occasionale	occasional	**speciale**	special
parte	part		

2. The Italian words add *a* or *o*.

lista	list	**costo**	cost
problema	problem	**liquido**	liquid
persona	person		

3. The Italian words have *a* or *o* where the English ones have *e*.

causa	cause	**favorito**	favorite
figura	figure	**minuto**	minute
medicina	medicine	**tubo**	tube
rosa	rose	**uso**	use

D. GENERAL SPELLING EQUIVALENTS

1. Italian *c (cc)* = English *k (ck)*:

franco	frank	**parco**	park
sacco	sack	**attacco**	attack

2. Italian *f* = English *ph*:

frase	phrase	**telefono**	telephone
fisico	physical	**fonico**	phonic

3. Italian *s (ss)* = English *x*:

esercizio	exercise	**Messico**	Mexico
esempio	example	**fisso**	fix

4. Italian *st* = English *xt*:

estensione	extension	**estremo**	extreme
esterno	external		

5. Italian *t* = English *th*:

autore	author	**teatro**	theatre
simpatia	sympathy	**teoria**	theory

6. Italian *z (zz)* = English *c*:

forza	force	**razza**	race

7. Italian *i* = English *y*:

stile	style	**sistema**	system
mistero	mystery	**ritmo**	rhythm

8. Italian *o* = English *ou:*

corte	court	**corso**	course
montagna	mountain		

9. Italian *-io* = English *-y:*

segretario	secretary	**territorio**	territory

10. Italian *-zione* = English *-tion:*

nazione	nation	**addizione**	addition

11. Italian *-o* = English *-al:*

interno	internal	**politico**	political
eterno	eternal		

12. Italian *-oso* = English *-ous:*

famoso	famous	**generoso**	generous
numeroso	numerous	**religioso**	religious

LESSON 5

A. NUMBERS 1–10

uno	one
due	two
tre	three
quattro	four
cinque	five
sei	six
sette	seven
otto	eight
nove	nine
dieci	ten

Uno più uno fa due.	One and one is two.
Uno più due fa tre.	One and two is three.
Due più due fanno quattro.	Two and two are four.
Due più tre fanno cinque.	Two and three are five.
Tre più tre fanno sei.	Three and three are six.
Tre più quattro fanno sette.	Three and four are seven.
Quattro più quattro fanno otto.	Four and four are eight.
Cinque più quattro fanno nove.	Five and four are nine.
Cinque più cinque fanno dieci.	Five and five are ten.

B. DAYS OF THE WEEK[1]

lunedì	Monday
martedì	Tuesday
mercoledì	Wednesday
giovedì	Thursday
venerdì	Friday
sabato	Saturday
domenica	Sunday

C. MONTHS OF THE YEAR

gennaio	January
febbraio	February
marzo	March
aprile	April
maggio	May
giugno	June
luglio	July
agosto	August
settembre	September
ottobre	October
novembre	November
dicembre	December

[1] The names of the days of the week and of the months are never capitalized.

D. SEASONS

primavera	spring
estate	summer
autunno	autumn
inverno	winter

E. NORTH, SOUTH, EAST, WEST

nord	north
sud	south
est	east
ovest	west

F. MORNING, NOON, AND NIGHT

mattina	morning
mezzogiorno	noon
pomeriggio	afternoon
sera	evening
notte	night

G. TODAY, YESTERDAY, TOMORROW

oggi	today
ieri	yesterday
domani	tomorrow

Oggi è venerdì.	Today is Friday.
Ieri era giovedì.	Yesterday was Thursday.
Domani è sabato.	Tomorrow is Saturday.

H. COLORS

rosso	red
blu	blue

verde	green
nero	black
bianco	white
giallo	yellow
marrone	brown (coffee color)
castagno	brown (chestnut color)
grigio	gray

QUIZ I

Try matching these two columns:

1. *venerdì*	a. January
2. *autunno*	b. summer
3. *giovedì*	c. June
4. *primavera*	d. winter
5. *otto*	e. October
6. *gennaio*	f. white
7. *inverno*	g. autumn
8. *verde*	h. Sunday
9. *giugno*	i. eight
10. *estate*	j. spring
11. *lunedì*	k. west
12. *quattro*	l. Thursday
13. *ottobre*	m. four
14. *domenica*	n. ten
15. *ovest*	o. red
16. *rosso*	p. black
17. *nero*	q. green
18. *dieci*	r. Friday
19. *bianco*	s. gray
20. *grigio*	t. Monday

ANSWERS

1—r; 2—g; 3—l; 4—j; 5—i; 6—a; 7—d; 8—q; 9—c;
10—b; 11—t; 12—m; 13—e; 14—h; 15—k; 16—o;
17—p; 18—n; 19—f; 20—s.

LESSON 6

A. GREETINGS

DI MATTINA	IN THE MORNING
buon	good
giorno	morning (day)[1]
Buon giorno.	Good morning.
Signor	Mr.
Rossi.	Rossi.
Buon giorno, signor Rossi.	Good morning, Mr. Rossi.
Salve	Hello *(polite)*
Ciao	Hello/Good-bye *(familiar)*
come	how
sta	are you
Come sta?	How are you? How do you do? *(polite)*
Come stai?	How are you? *(familiar)*
molto	very
bene	well
Molto bene.	Very well.
grazie	thank you, thanks
Molto bene, grazie.	Very well, thank you.
E Lei?[2]	And you? *(polite)*
E tu?	And you? *(familiar)*
bene	fine
Bene, grazie.	Fine, thank you.
Arrivederci.	Good-bye.
Ciao.	Bye. *(familiar)*

[1] Words in parentheses are literal translations.
[2] Italian has both a polite, formal form of "you" *(Lei)* and an informal, familiar form *(tu)*. Use *tu* when talking to family, good friends, pets or children. In other situations, it's better to err on the side of politeness and use *Lei*.

DI SERA	IN THE EVENING
buona	good
sera	evening
Buona sera.	Good evening.
Buona sera, signora Rossi.	Good evening, Mrs. Rossi.
Buona notte.	Good night.
Buona notte, signorina Rossi.	Good night, Miss Rossi.

Note: The Italian word for "sir" or "Mr." is *signore,* but when it is used immediately preceding a name, the *e* is dropped.

Buon giorno, signor Rossi.
Buon giorno, signore.

B. HOW'S THE WEATHER?

Che tempo fa oggi?	What's the weather today?
Fa bel tempo.	It's nice (beautiful weather).
Fa brutto tempo.	It's awful (ugly weather).
Fa freddo.	It's cold.
Fa fresco.	It's cool.
Fa caldo.	It's hot.
Piove.	It's raining.
Nevica.	It's snowing.
C'è il sole.	It's sunny.
È nuvoloso.	It's cloudy.
Tira vento.	It's windy.

QUIZ 2

1. *mattina*
2. *signora*
3. *E Lei?*
4. *molto bene*

a. Good evening.
b. How are you? *(polite)*
c. Miss
d. morning

5. *Buon giorno.*   e. Thank you.
6. *Buona notte.*   f. Madam or Mrs.
7. *Come sta?*   g. How are you? *(familiar)*
8. *Piove.*   h. sir or Mr.
9. *Grazie.*   i. What's the weather
                                today?
10. *Come stai?*   j. Good morning.
11. *signorina*   k. It's nice.
12. *Buona sera.*   l. And you? *(polite)*
13. *Que tempo fa oggi?*   m. very well
14. *signore*   n. It's raining.
15. *Fa bel tempo.*   o. Good night.

ANSWERS

1—d; 2—f; 3—l; 4—m; 5—j; 6—o; 7—b; 8—n; 9—e;
10—g; 11—c; 12—a; 13—i; 14—h; 15—k.

C. WORD STUDY

classe	class
considerabile	considerable
differenza	difference
elemento	element
gloria	glory
operazione	operation
madre	mother
padre	father

LESSON 7

A. WHERE IS . . . ?

dove	where
è	is
dov'è *(dove è)*	where is
Dov'è un albergo?	Where is a hotel?

buon ristorante	good restaurant
Dov'è un buon ristorante?	Where's a good restaurant?
dov'è	where is
Dov'è?	Where is it?
Dov'è il telefono?	Where's the telephone?
Dov'è il ristorante?	Where's the restaurant?
Dov'è la toilette?	Where's the bathroom?
Dov'è la stazione?	Where's the train station?
Dov'è l'ufficio postale?	Where's the post office?

B. CAN YOU TELL ME . . . ?

può dirmi[1]	can you tell me *(polite)*
Può dirmi dov'è un albergo?	Can you tell me where there is a hotel?
Può dirmi dov'è un buon ristorante?	Can you tell me where there is a good restaurant?
Può dirmi dov'è il telefono?	Can you tell me where the telephone is?
Può dirmi dov'è la stazione?	Can you tell me where the train station is?
Può dirmi dov'è l'ufficio postale?	Can you tell me where the post office is?

QUIZ 3

1. *Dov'è un albergo?*
2. *Dov'è il telefono?*
3. *Può dirmi Lei . . . ?*

a. Where's the telephone?
b. Can you tell me where the train station is?
c. Can you tell me . . . ?

[1] Note that the question *Può dirmi . . . ?* (Can you tell me?) can be used with or without the pronoun *Lei*.

4. *Può dirmi dov'è la stazione?*   d. the post office

5. *l'ufficio postale*   e. Where is a hotel?

ANSWERS

1—e; 2—a; 3—c; 4—b; 5—d.

C. DO YOU HAVE . . . ?

Ha . . . ?	Do you have . . . ? *(polite)*
Hai . . . ?	Do you have . . . ? *(familiar)*
denaro	(any) money
sigarette	(any) cigarettes
fiammiferi	(any) matches
Ho bisogno di . . .	I need . . .
carta	(some) paper
una matita	a pencil
una penna	a pen
un francobollo	a stamp
dentifricio	toothpaste
un asciugamano	a towel
sapone	soap
Dove posso comprare . . . ?	Where can I buy . . . ?
un dizionario italiano	an Italian dictionary
un dizionario inglese-italiano	an English-Italian dictionary
un libro in inglese	an English book
degli abiti	some clothes

D. IN A RESTAURANT

(prima) colazione	breakfast
pranzo	lunch
cena	dinner

Che cosa desidera?	What will you have? (What do you wish?)
Che cosa desidera mangiare?	What would you like to eat?
Mi dia il menu, per favore.	Give me the menu, please.
Posso avere il menu, per favore?	May I have the menu, please?

Mi porti . . .   Bring me . . .

un po' di pane	some bread
pane e burro	bread and butter
della minestra	some soup
della carne	some meat
del manzo	some beef
una bistecca	a steak
del prosciutto	some ham
del pesce	some fish
del pollo	some chicken
delle uova	some eggs
della verdura	some vegetables
delle patate	some potatoes
dell'insalata	some salad
dell'acqua	some water
del vino	some wine
della birra	some beer
del latte	some milk
caffè latte	coffee with milk
dello zucchero	some sugar
del sale	some salt
del pepe	some pepper
della frutta	some fruit
dei dolci	some dessert

Mi porti . . .   Bring me . . .

una tazza di caffè	a cup of coffee
una tazza di tè	a cup of tea

un tovagliolo	a napkin
un cucchiaio	a spoon
un cucchiaino	a teaspoon
un coltello	a knife
un piatto	a plate
un bicchiere	a glass

Desidero . . .	I would like . . .
un po' di frutta	some fruit (assorted)
una bottiglia di vino	a bottle of wine
un' altra bottiglia di vino	another bottle of wine
un po' di più	a little more
un po' più di pane	a little more bread
un po' più di carne	a little more meat

Il conto, per favore.	The check, please.

QUIZ 4

1. *carne*	a. fish
2. *patate*	b. water
3. *acqua*	c. vegetables
4. *Che cosa desidera?*	d. I need soap.
5. *uova*	e. The check, please.
6. *pollo*	f. breakfast
7. *pesce*	g. a spoon
8. *una bottiglia di vino*	h. coffee with milk
9. *Ho bisogno di sapone.*	i. What will you have?
10. *Mi porti un po' più dì pane.*	j. dessert
11. *caffelatte*	k. meat
12. *zucchero*	l. a knife
13. *verdura*	m. eggs
14. *una tazza di tè*	n. Bring me a little more bread.
15. *un piatto*	o. chicken
16. *un coltello*	p. a cup of tea
17. *dolci*	q. a plate

18. *prima colazione*   r. sugar
19. *un cucchiaio*   s. a bottle of wine
20. *Il conto, per favore.*   t. potatoes

ANSWERS

1—k; 2—t; 3—b; 4—i; 5—m; 6—o; 7—a; 8—s; 9—d;
10—n; 11—h; 12—r; 13—c; 14—p; 15—q; 16—l; 17—j;
18—f; 19—g; 20—e.

LESSON 8

A. TO SPEAK: *PARLARE*

io parlo	I speak
tu parli	you speak *(familiar)*
lui parla	he speaks
lei parla	she speaks
Lei parla	you speak *(polite)*
noi parliamo	we speak
voi parlate	you speak *(plural)*
loro parlano	they speak *(masc. or fem.)*
Loro parlano	you speak *(formal plural)*

NOTES

1. These forms, which make up the present tense, translate into the English as "I speak," "I am speaking," and
   "I do speak." *Parlare* is an *-are* verb (also called a verb
   of the first conjugation) because its infinitive form (to
   speak) ends in *-are*. There are many other common
   -are verbs that are conjugated like *parlare:*

lavorare	to work	**mangiare**	to eat
studiare	to study	**cucinare**	to cook

2. *Tu,* you, is used to address people you know very well
   (whom you call by their first names in English—rela-

tives, close friends, children, pets, etc.). The plural for *tu* is *voi*. *Lei,* you, is used to address people you're meeting for the first time or don't know very well, acquaintances, superiors, and elders. The plural for *Lei* is *Loro,* but in conversation you will probably hear *voi* used as the plural for both *tu* and *Lei*.

3. Notice that there are six endings that indicate the person speaking or spoken about, without need of pronouns:

Singular:

-*o* indicates the speaker (I)

-*i* indicates the person spoken to (you). It is used only with someone you know well.

-*a* indicates someone or something spoken about (he, she, it), or else you *(polite)*.

Plural:

-*iamo* indicates several speakers (we).

-*ate* is the plural form for *tu*. *Voi* is also used to address one or more persons in a polite way.

-*ano* indicates they (both masculine and feminine). *Loro* is also used to address one or more persons in a formal way.

4. Notice that the verb form with *Lei, lui, lei* is the same: *parla*.

5. Notice that *lui* or *lei* is used with the verb form *parla,* depending on whether you are referring to a man or a woman:

lui parla   he is speaking
lei parla   she is speaking

6. The subject pronouns *lei, loro,* and the direct object pronouns *le, la, li* when they mean "you" are often capitalized to emphasize the idea of respect toward a person—for instance, when writing a formal letter or addressing someone in a respectful way. They are capitalized in this program for clarity.

B. The and A

1. The

MASCULINE

Singular:		Plural:	
il libro	the book	**i libri**	the books
lo studio	the study	**gli studi**	the studies
l'esercizio	the exercise	**gli esercizi**	the exercises

FEMININE

Singular:		Plural:	
la donna	the woman	**le donne**	the women
l'agenzia	the agency	**le agenzie**	the agencies

Notice the different forms used in Italian for the single English word *the*. In Italian, words are either masculine or feminine. When they refer to males or females, you know which group of articles to use, but in the case of other nouns, you have to learn whether the noun is masculine or feminine. The masculine article *il* and its plural form *i* are used before masculine nouns beginning with a consonant. The masculine article *lo* and its plural form *gli* are used before masculine nouns beginning with a vowel or a *z*, or *s* plus another consonant, or the consonant combination *gn*. When used before a vowel, *lo* is elided to *l'*; the plural does not elide unless the following word begins with an *i*. The feminine article *la* and its plural form *le* are used before feminine nouns; however, before vowels, *la* is also elided to *l'*.

2. A (An)

MASCULINE		FEMININE	
un ragazzo	a boy	**una ragazza**	a girl
uno zero	a zero	**un'amica**	a friend (*fem.*)

The indefinite article (a, an) has the form *un* before masculine nouns beginning with vowels and most consonants. It takes the form *uno* before masculine nouns beginning with *z*, or *s* plus another consonant, or the combination *gn*. The feminine form is *una*, eliding to *un'* before a vowel.

QUIZ 5

1. *io*	a. they speak
2. *noi*	b. she is speaking
3. *tu parli*	c. she
4. *lui*	d. you *(plural)*
5. *loro parlano*	e. I
6. *voi*	f. you speak
7. *tu*	g. he
8. *lei*	h. we speak
9. *noi parliamo*	i. you *(fam. sing.)*
10. *lei parla*	j. we

ANSWERS

1—e; 2—j; 3—f; 4—g; 5—a; 6—d; 7—i; 8—c; 9—h; 10—b.

C. CONTRACTIONS

di + il = del (of the)	*a + il = al* (to the)
di + lo = dello	*a + lo = allo*
di + la = della	*a + la = alla*
di + l' = dell'	*a + l' = all'*
di + i = dei	*a + i = ai*
di + gli = degli	*a + gli = agli*
di + le = delle	*a + le = alle*
con + il = col (with the)	*su + il = sul* (on the)
con + i = coi	*su + la = sulla*
	su + lo = sullo
	su + gli = sugli

D. PLURALS OF NOUNS

As a general rule, nouns ending in *o* are masculine, nouns ending in *a* are feminine, and nouns ending in *e* can be either masculine or feminine.

All masculine nouns (ending either in *o* or *e*) form their plural with an *i*.

Feminine nouns that end in *a* in the singular form their plural with an *e*. Feminine nouns that end in *e* in the singular form their plural with an *i*.

il piatto	the plate	**i piatti**	the plates
il cuore	the heart	**i cuori**	the hearts
la rosa	the rose	**le rose**	the roses
la valle	the valley	**le valli**	the valleys

E. ADJECTIVES

There are two groups of adjectives:

1. Those that have four endings:

caro *(masc. sing.)*   **cara** *(fem. sing.)*
cari *(masc. plur.)*   **care** *(fem. plur.)*

2. Those that have only two endings:

gentile *(masc. and fem. sing.)*
gentili *(masc. and fem. plur.)*

Study these examples:

un caro amico	a dear friend *(masc.)*
una cara amica	a dear friend *(fem.)*
dei cari amici	some dear friends *(masc.)*
delle care amiche	some dear friends *(fem.)*
un uomo gentile	a kind man *(masc.)*

una donna gentile	a kind woman *(fem.)*
degli uomini gentili[1]	some kind men *(masc.)*
delle donne gentili[1]	some kind women *(fem.)*

The adjective always agrees with its noun. When an adjective is used alone, its ending usually tells you whether it refers to a singular or plural, feminine or masculine noun:

È italiano.	He is Italian.
È italiana.	She is Italian.
Sono italiani.	They are Italian.
Sono italiane.	They are Italian. *(fem.)*

NOTES

Only proper names and geographical nouns are capitalized in Italian. Names of nationalities are capitalized only when used as nouns and referring to a person. When used as adjectives, or to refer to a language, they are not capitalized.

Examples:

un libro italiano	an Italian book
Ho incontrato un Italiano.	I met an Italian.
Loro parlano italiano.	They speak Italian.

F. Possession

English -'s or -s' is translated by *di* (of):

il libro di Giovanni	John's book (the book of John)
i libri dei ragazzi	the boys' books (the books of the boys)
il libro di Maria	Maria's book
i libri delle ragazze	the girls' books

---

[1] Note that some adjectives come before the noun they modify, and some after. See Section 9 in the Summary of Italian Grammar.

G. ASKING A QUESTION

To ask a question you can either put the subject after the verb:

Ha mangiato Lei?   Have you eaten?

or preserve the same word order and raise your voice at the end of the sentence to show that it is a question. Compare:

Lei ha mangiato.   You have eaten.
Lei ha mangiato?   Have you eaten?

H. NOT

The word for "not" is *non*. It comes before the verb.

Non vedo Marco.   I don't see Mark.
Non sono italiana.   I'm not Italian.

REVIEW QUIZ I

1. *Buon* _____ (morning), *signora Rossi.*
   a. *domani*
   b. *giorno*
   c. *grazie*
2. *Può dirmi* _____ (where's) *l'ufficio postale?*
   a. *dov'è*
   b. *buono*
   c. *lì*
3. _____ (Bring me) *un po' di pane.*
   a. *Mangiare*
   b. *Sera*
   c. *Mi porti*
4. *caffelatte con* _____ (sugar)
   a. *tè*
   b. *vino*
   c. *zucchero*
5. *un po'* _____ (more) *di carne*
   a. *più*
   b. *tazza*
   c. *ancora*

6. *il sette* _____ (January)
   a. *marzo*
   b. *gennaio*
   c. *agosto*

7. _____ (Wednesday), *cinque settembre*
   a. *inverno*
   b. *sabato*
   c. *mercoledì*

8. _____ (How) *sta?*
   a. *Grazie*
   b. *Come*
   c. *Sera*

9. *Buona* _____ (evening), *signorina Rossi.*
   a. *fino*
   b. *sera*
   c. *io*

10. *Desidero una bottiglia di* _____ (wine).
    a. *latte*
    b. *vino*
    c. *acqua*

ANSWERS

1—b; 2—a; 3—c; 4—c; 5—a; 6—b; 7—c; 8—b; 9—b;
10—b.

LESSON 9

A. MAY I INTRODUCE . . . ?

Buon giorno.	Good morning.
Buon giorno, signore.	Good morning, sir.
Come sta?	How are you? *(polite)*
Molto bene, grazie e Lei? Lei E americano?	Very well, thanks, and how are you? Are you American?
Sì, signore.	Yes, sir.
Parla italiano?	Do you speak Italian?
Un po'.	A little.
La presento alla mia amica, signorina Rossi.	Let me introduce you to my friend, Miss Rossi.
Posso presentarLe la mia amica, signorina Rossi?	May I introduce my friend, Miss Rossi?
Molto piacere di conoscerLa.	Pleased to meet you. (Much pleasure in knowing you.)
Felice di conoscerLa.	I'm glad (happy) to meet (know) you.
Il piacere è mio.	The pleasure is mine.
Mi permetta che mi presenti: Sono Giovanni Rossi.	Allow me to introduce myself: I'm John Rossi.

B. HOW ARE THINGS?

Buon giorno, Paolo!	Hello, Paul!
Ciao, Giovanni!	Hi, John!
Come stai?	How are you? *(familiar)*
Come vanno le cose?	How are things? (How go things?)

Bene e tu?	Fine, and how are you? *(fam.)*
che c'è	what is there
di nuovo	(of) new
Che c'è di nuovo?	What's new?
niente	nothing
di particolare	in (of) particular
Niente di particolare.	Nothing in particular.
che	what
mi racconti	do (you) tell me
Che mi racconti?	What's new?
Poche cose.	(Few things.) Not much.
Non molto.	Not much.

C. GOOD-BYE

è stato	it's been
un vero piacere	a real pleasure
È stato un vero piacere.	It's been a real pleasure.
il piacere	the pleasure
Il piacere è stato mio.	The pleasure was mine.
Arrivederci ad un altro giorno.	Good-bye until another day.
A presto.	See you soon.
A più tardi.	See you later.
Buona notte.	Good night.
Ciao!	Good-bye./Hello. *(familiar)*
A dopo!	See you later!
Ci vediamo.	See you.
Alla prossima.	Until next (time).
A domani.	See you tomorrow.

QUIZ 6

1. *Come stai?*   a. Nothing in particular.
2. *Arrivederci.*   b. Allow me to introduce
                         you to my friend.

3. *Buona notte.*	c. See you soon.
4. *Buon giorno, Giovanni.*	d. Hello, John.
5. *Niente di particolare.*	e. Pleased to meet you.
6. *Mi permetta di presentarLa al mio amico.*	f. How are you?
7. *A presto.*	g. Good night.
8. *nuovo*	h. to meet you
9. *Molto piacere di conoscerLa*	i. new
10. *conoscerLa*	j. Good-bye.

ANSWERS

1—f; 2—j; 3—g; 4—d; 5—a; 6—b; 7—c; 8—i; 9—e;
10—h.

LESSON 10

A. To Be or Not to Be: *Essere*[1]

Study these forms of the important irregular verb *essere,*
"to be."

io sono	I am
tu sei	you are *(familiar)*
Lei è	you are *(polite)*
lui è	he is
lei è	she is
noi siamo	we are
voi siete	you are *(plural)*
Loro sono	you are *(formal plur.)*
loro sono	they are
Lui è dottore.	He is a doctor.
Lui è scrittore.	He is a writer.
Lui è italiano.	He's Italian.

[1] See Section 43 of the Grammar Summary for more information about *essere.*

Il libro è rosso.	The book is red.
Lei è giovane.	She is young.
Il ghiaccio è freddo.	Ice is cold.
Lui è intelligente.	He's intelligent.
Lei è incantevole.	She's charming.

Sono io.	It's me.
Di dov'è Lei?	Where are you from? *(polite)*
Di dove sei?	Where are you from? *(fam.)*
Io sono italiano.	I'm Italian.
Di cosa è fatto?	What is it made of?
È fatto di legno.	It's made of wood.
È d'argento.	It's silver.
Di chi è questo?	Whose is this?
Il libro è del signor Rossi.	The book belongs to Mr. Rossi.
È l'una.	It's one o'clock.
Sono le due.	It's two o'clock.
Sono le nove e dieci.	It's ten past nine.

Sono otto euro la dozzina.	They are eight euros a dozen.
Sono cinque euro l'uno.	They are five euros each.
È tardi.	It's late.
È presto.	It's early.
È necessario.	It's necessary.
È un peccato.	It's a pity.
Non è vero?	Right? (Isn't it true?)

The verb *stare* means "to stay, to remain," but in certain expressions, such as expressions of health, it can mean "to be."

io sto	I stay (am)
tu stai	you stay (are)
lui sta	he stays (is)
noi stiamo	we stay (are)
voi state	you stay (are)
loro stanno	they stay (are)

Come sta?[1] How are you? *(polite)*
Sto bene. I am well.

QUIZ 7

1. *Lui è intelligente.* a. Whose is this?
2. *È un peccato.* b. Where are you from?
3. *Lui è dottore.* c. they are
4. *io sono* d. He's a doctor.
5. *È l'una.* e. It's early.
6. *noi siamo* f. He's Italian.
7. *È fatto di legno.* g. He's intelligent.
8. *Di dov'è Lei?* h. It's a pity.
9. *È presto.* i. I am
10. *Io sono stanco.* j. It's one o'clock.
11. *loro sono* k. It's made of wood.
12. *Di chi è questo?* l. we are
13. *È tardi.* m. I'm tired.
14. *Lui è italiano.* n. It's late.

ANSWERS

1—g; 2—h; 3—d; 4—i; 5—j; 6—l; 7—k; 8—b; 9—e;
10—m; 11—c; 12—a; 13—n; 14—f.

B. It Is . . .

È . . . It is . . .
È vero. It's true.
Questo non è vero. This isn't true.
Questo non è così. This isn't so.
È così. Così è. It's so. That's the way it is.
È male. It's bad.
È molto male. It's very bad.
È certo. It's certain.
È grande. It's big.

---

[1] See Section 44 of the Grammar Summary for the verb *stare*.

È piccolo.	It's small.
È caro.	It's expensive.
È economico.	It's affordable.
È vicino.	It's near.
È lontano.	It's far.
È difficile.	It's difficult.
È facile.	It's easy.
È poco. Non è molto.	It's a little. It's not much.
È molto poco.	It's very little.
È molto.	It's a lot.
È abbastanza.	It's enough.
Non è abbastanza.	It's not enough.
È qui.	It's here.
È lì.	It's there.
È tuo.	It's yours. *(familiar)*
È Suo.	It's yours. *(polite)*
È mio.	It's mine.
È nostro.	It's ours.
È per te.	It's for you. *(familiar)*
È per Lei.	It's for you. *(polite)*

QUIZ 8

1. *È molto.*
2. *È facile.*
3. *È vicino.*
4. *È abbastanza.*
5. *Questo non è vero.*
6. *È male.*
7. *È piccolo.*
8. *È vero.*
9. *È mio.*
10. *È qui.*

a. It's enough.
b. This isn't true.
c. It's bad.
d. It's near.
e. It's mine.
f. It's true.
g. It's here.
h. It's small.
i. It's easy.
j. It's a lot.

ANSWERS

1—j; 2—i; 3—d; 4—a; 5—b; 6—c; 7—h; 8—f; 9—e;
10—g.

C. To Have and Have Not: *Avere*

TO HAVE

io ho	I have
tu hai	you have *(familiar)*
Lei ha	you have *(polite)*
lui ha	he has
noi abbiamo	we have
voi avete	you have
loro hanno	they have

NOT TO HAVE

io non ho	I don't have
tu non hai	you don't have *(familiar)*
Lei non ha	you don't have *(polite)*
lui non ha	he doesn't have
noi non abbiamo	we don't have
voi non avete	you don't have
loro non hanno	they don't have

Study these expressions with *avere*.

Io ho tempo.	I have time.
Io non ho tempo.	I don't have any time.
Lui non ha amici.	He doesn't have any friends.
Ha una sigaretta?	Do you have a cigarette?
Io ho fame.	I'm hungry. (I have hunger.)
Ho sete. (Io ho sete.)	I'm thirsty. (I have thirst.)
Ho freddo. (Io ho freddo.)	I'm cold. (I have cold.)
Ho caldo. (Io ho caldo.)	I'm hot. (I have heat.)
Ho ragione.	I'm right. (I have reason.)

QUIZ 9

1. *noi abbiamo*	a. I'm cold.
2. *lui non ha*	b. we have
3. *Io non ho tempo.*	c. he doesn't have
4. *Ho freddo.*	d. I'm hungry.
5. *Io ho fame.*	e. I don't have time.

ANSWERS

1—b; 2—c; 3—e; 4—a; 5—d.

LESSON 11

A. I ONLY KNOW A LITTLE ITALIAN

1. *Parlare:* to speak

Parla italiano?	Do you speak Italian? *(polite)*
Lei parla italiano?	Do you speak Italian? *(polite)*
Sì, un po'.	Yes, a little.
Molto poco.	Very little.
Non molto bene.	Not very well.
Io parlo italiano.	I speak Italian.
Lo parlo male.	I speak it poorly.
Io non lo parlo molto bene.	I don't speak it very well.
Il suo amico parla italiano?	Does your friend speak Italian?
No, il mio amico non parla italiano.	No, my friend doesn't speak Italian.

2. *Conoscere:* to know; to be acquainted with

Io conosco solo poche parole.	I know only a few words.

3. *Leggere:* to read; *Dire:* to say

Lo leggo ma non lo parlo.	I read it, but I don't speak it.
Che cosa ha detto?	What did you say? *(polite)*

4. *Capire:* to understand

Capisce l'italiano?	Do you understand Italian?
Sì, capisco l'italiano.	Yes, I understand Italian.
Lo capisco ma non lo parlo.	I understand it, but I don't speak it.
Lo leggo ma non lo parlo.	I read it, but I don't speak it.
No, io non capisco l'italiano.	No, I don't understand Italian.
Io non capisco molto bene l'italiano.	I don't understand Italian very well.
Non lo pronuncio molto bene.	I don't pronounce it very well.
Mi manca la pratica.	I lack practice.
Ho bisogno di pratica.	I need practice.
Lei mi capisce?	Do you understand me?
Io La capisco.	I understand you.
Io non La capisco molto bene.	I don't understand you very well.
Lei parla troppo in fretta.	You speak too fast. (You speak in too much of a hurry.)
Lei parla troppo veloce.	You are speaking too fast.
Non parli così in fretta.	Don't speak so fast. *(polite)*
Parli più lentamente.	Speak more slowly. *(polite)*
Per favore, parli più lentamente.	Please speak a little more slowly. *(polite)*
Mi scusi ma non La capisco.	Excuse me, but I don't understand.
Non L'ho capita.	I didn't understand you.
Per favore me lo ripeta.	Please say it again (to me). *(polite)*
Mi capisce ora?	Do you understand me now? *(polite)*
Oh, ora capisco.	Oh, now I understand.

5. *Scrivere:* to write; *Significare:* to mean, to denote

Che cosa significa in italiano?	What does it mean in Italian?
Come si dice "Thanks" in italiano?	How do you say "Thanks" in Italian?
Come si scrive questa parola?	How do you spell (write) that word?
Per favore me la scriva.	Please write it down for me. *(polite)*

B. A BRIEF CONVERSATION WITH A STRANGER

Buon giorno, signore.	Good morning, sir.
Buon giorno.	Good morning.
Lei parla italiano?	Do you speak Italian?
Sì, parlo italiano.	Yes, I speak Italian.
Non parlo inglese.	I don't speak English.
Lei è italiano?	Are you Italian?
Sì, sono italiano.	Yes, I am Italian.
Da quanto tempo è negli Stati Uniti?	How long have you been in the United States?
Da tre mesi.	For three months.
Imparerà presto l'inglese.	You'll soon learn English.
Imparerà l'inglese in poco tempo. Non è molto difficile.	You'll learn English in no time (little time). It's not very hard.
È più difficile di quanto creda.	It's harder than you think.
Forse ha ragione.	You are probably right.
È più facile per noi imparare l'italiano che per voi l'inglese.	It is easier for us to learn Italian than for you (to learn) English.
Lei parla italiano molto bene.	You speak Italian very well.

Italian	English
Ho vissuto in Italia per diversi anni.	I lived in Italy for several years.
Ha un'ottima pronuncia.	You have (an) excellent pronunciation.
Molte grazie, ma mi manca la pratica.	Thank you, but I need (lack) practice.
Ho bisogno di pratica.	I need practice.
Adesso devo andare. Il mio treno sta per partire.	I have to go now. My train's about to leave.
Buona fortuna e buon viaggio.	Good luck and have a nice trip.
Altrettanto.	The same to you.
Addio.	Farewell.

C. EXCUSE ME AND THANK YOU

Italian	English
Mi scusi.	Pardon me. Excuse me.
Le chiedo scusa.	I beg your pardon.
Per favore, ripeta.	Please repeat.
Mi vuole fare il favore di ripetere?	Will you do me the favor of repeating it?
Con piacere.	With pleasure. Gladly.
Con molto piacere.	With the greatest pleasure.
Sono a Sua disposizione.	I'm at your disposal.
Che cosa posso fare per Lei?	What (thing) can I do for you?
Lei è molto gentile.	You are very kind.
Lei è molto cortese.	You are very kind. (You are very courteous.)
Grazie.	Thanks.
Molte grazie.	Many thanks.
Grazie infinite.	Thanks a lot. (Infinite thanks.)
Mille grazie.	Thanks very much. (A thousand thanks.)

Di niente.   Don't mention it. (Of
                                     nothing.)
Non c'è di che.   Don't mention it.
Niente affatto.   It's nothing. (Nothing at all.)

QUIZ 10

1. *Lo comprendo ma non*   a. Do you speak Italian?
   lo parlo.
2. *Mi comprende ora?*   b. I need practice.
3. *Non lo parlo molto bene.* c. Don't mention it.
4. *Lei è molto gentile.*   d. What did you say?
5. *Come si scrive questa*   e. Say it again.
   parola?
6. *Lei parla italiano?*   f. Not very well.
7. *Ho bisogno di practica.*   g. I didn't understand very
                                  well.
8. *Non c'è di che.*   h. I understand it, but I
                                  don't speak it.
9. *Me lo ripeta.*   i. Speak more slowly.
10. *Non molto bene.*   j. I don't speak it very well.
11. *Parli più lentamente.*   k. How do you say
                                  "Thanks" in Italian?
12. *Mille grazie.*   l. You are very kind.
13. *Che cosa ha detto?*   m. Do you understand me
                                  now?
14. *Come si dice "Thanks"*   n. How do you spell this
    in italiano?   word?
15. *Non ho capito bene.*   o. Thank you very much.

ANSWERS
1—h; 2—m; 3—j; 4—l; 5—n; 6—a; 7—b; 8—c; 9—e;
10—f; 11—i; 12—o; 13—d; 14—k; 15—g.

D. WORD STUDY

commedia	comedy
costante	constant
contrario	contrary
desiderio	desire
lungo	long
opera	opera
semplice	simple
venditore	vendor

LESSON 12

A. THIS AND THAT (DEMONSTRATIVE PRONOUNS AND ADJECTIVES)

Study the following expressions using the demonstratives *questo* and *quello*.[1]

Dammi questo.	Give me this one. (*masc.*)
Dammi questa.	Give me this one. (*fem.*)
Dammi questi.	Give me these. (*masc.*)
Dammi queste.	Give me these. (*fem.*)
Dammi quello.	Give me that one. (*masc.*)
Dammi quella.	Give me that one. (*fem.*)
Dammi quelli.	Give me those. (*masc.*)
Dammi quelle.	Give me those. (*fem.*)
Dammi quello là.	Give me that one (*masc.*) over there.
Dammi quella là.	Give me that one (*fem.*) over there.
Dammi quelli là.	Give me those (*masc.*) over there.

[1] See also Section 21 in the Summary of Italian Grammar.

Dammi quelle là.   Give me those *(fem.)* over
                                    there.

When *questo* and *quello* are used as adjectives preceding
nouns, the forms of *questo* are the same as above, but *quello*
has a different set of endings:

questo ragazzo	this boy
questa signora	this woman
quel signore là	that gentleman over there
quella signora	that woman
quello sbaglio	that mistake
quei vicini	those neighbors
quegli studenti	those students

QUIZ 11

1. *Dammi questi.*	a. Give me those over there.
2. *questo*	b. that one over there
3. *Dammi quella.*	c. this woman
4. *questo ragazzo*	d. this one
5. *quello*	e. that gentleman over there
6. *quei vicini*	f. this boy
7. *Dammi quelli là.*	g. Give me these.
8. *quello là*	h. that one
9. *questa signora*	i. those neighbors
10. *quel signore là*	j. Give me that one. *(fem.)*

ANSWERS

1—g; 2—d; 3—j; 4—f; 5—h; 6—i; 7—a; 8—b; 9—c;
10—e.

B. MORE OR LESS

1. More

più piano	more slowly
più difficile	more difficult

più facile	easier
più lontano	farther
più vicino	nearer
più di quello	more than that
più di un anno	more than a year

2. Less

meno piano	less slowly
meno difficile	less difficult
meno facile	less easy
meno lontano	less far, not so far
meno vicino	less near, not so near
meno di quello	less than that
meno di un anno	less than a year

C. AND, OR, BUT

1. *e* "and"

Roberto e Giovanni sono fratelli.	Robert and John are brothers.

ed is used instead of *e* before nouns beginning with a vowel:

Roberto ed Andrea sono fratelli.	Robert and Andrew are brothers.

2. *o* "or"

cinque o sei giorni	five or six days
sette o otto ore	seven or eight hours

3. *ma* "but"

Lui non è francese, ma inglese.	He is not French but English.
Lui non viene oggi, ma domani.	He is not coming today but tomorrow.

D. WORD STUDY

catena	chain
lettera	letter
completo	complete
creare	create
eterno	eternal
fontana	fountain
ufficiale	officer

QUIZ 12

1.	*inglese*	a.	five or six days
2.	*e*	b.	more than that
3.	*ma*	c.	seven or eight hours
4.	*più facile*	d.	English
5.	*fratello*	e.	but
6.	*cinque o sei giorni*	f.	tomorrow
7.	*meno piano*	g.	easier
8.	*più di quello*	h.	and
9.	*domani*	i.	less slowly
10.	*sette o otto ore*	j.	brother

ANSWERS

1—d; 2—h; 3—e; 4—g; 5—j; 6—a; 7—i; 8—b; 9—f;
10—c.

LESSON 13

A. WHERE?

Dove?	Where?
Dov'è?	Where is it?
Dove si trova?	Where is it located (found)?
Qui.	Here.
Lì.	There.
All'angolo.	On the corner.

È in Via Condotti.	It's on the Via Condotti. (*via* = street)
Si trova in Via Condotti.[1]	It's located on the Via Condotti.
È in Piazza Venezia.	It's on Piazza Venezia.
Si trova in Piazza Venezia.	(*piazza* = square)
È in Viale Mazzini.	It's on Viale Mazzini.
Si trova in Viale Mazzini.	(*viale* = avenue)
Per dove? Per quale strada?	Which way?
Per questa strada. Per questa via.	This way.
Per quella strada.	That way.
Come si arriva lì?	How do you get there?
Dov'è questo posto?	Where's that place?
È qui.	It's here.
È proprio qui.	It's right here.
È lì.	It's there.

B. HERE AND THERE

Dov'è il libro?	Where's the book?
È qui.	It's here.
È proprio qui.	It's right here.
È lì.	It's there (where you are).
È la.	It's over there (distant from both of us).
Dov'è Lei?	Where are you?
Sono qui.	Here I am.
Lui è qui.	He is here.
Lui si trova qui.	He's here.
Lui è lì.	He's there.
Eccolo che va via.	There he is, going away.
Eccolo che se ne va.	

[1] *È* and *si trova* are two interchangeable ways of indicating the location of something.

È lì, da qualche parte.	It's somewhere over there.
Lo metta qui.	Put it here. *(polite)*
Lo metta lì.	Put it there. *(polite)*
Mi aspetti qui.	Wait for me here. *(polite)*
Mi aspetti lì.	Wait for me there. *(polite)*
Venga qui.	Come here. *(polite)*
Eccolo che viene.	Here he comes.
Vada lì.	Go there. *(polite)*
Fino a lì.	As far as there.
Qui intorno.	Around here.
Qui vicino.	Near here.
Lì in Italia.	Over there in Italy.
Qui in America.	Here in America.
Dove abita lui?	Where does he live?
Lui abita lì.	He lives there.
Io spero di vederlo lì.	I expect to see him there.
Lei è lì.	She's there.
Giovanni abita qui?	Does John live here?
È qui.	It's here. This is the place.
Non è qui.	It's not here.
È lì.	It's there.
Prenda questa strada.	Go this way. (Take this street.) *(pol.)*
Prenda quella strada.	Go that way. (Take that street.) *(pol.)*
Venga per questa strada.	Come this way. (Come by this street.) *(polite)*
Vada di lì.	Go that way. *(polite)*
Ho i libri qui.	I have the books here.
Cosa hai lì?	What do you have there?
Sei lì?	Are you there?

C. To the Right, etc.

Dov'è?	Where is it?
A destra.	To the right.

A sinistra.	To the left.
Giri a destra. Svolti a destra.	Turn to your right. *(polite)*
Giri a sinistra. Svolti a sinistra.	Turn to your left. *(polite)*
Vada sempre avanti.	Go straight ahead. *(polite)*
Continua (diritto) dritto.	Continue straight ahead. *(pol.)*
È (diritto) dritto.	It's straight ahead.
È proprio di fronte.	It's directly opposite.
È sopra.	It's above.
È sotto.	It's below.
È all' angolo.	It's at the corner.

D. NEAR AND FAR

qui vicino	near here
molto vicino	very near
a pochi passi da qui	a few steps from here
vicino al paese	near the town
vicino al parco	near the park
vicino alla chiesa	next to the church
È lontano?	Is it far?
È lontano da qui?	Is it far from here?
È più lontano.	It's farther.
È un po' più lontano.	It's a little farther.
Quanto è lontano da qui?	How far is it from here?
È vicino.	It's near.
Non è troppo lontano.	It's not too far.
È lontano da qui?	Is it far from here?
È molto lontano.	It's very far.
Non è molto lontano.	It's not too far.
Si trova a duecento metri da qui.	It's two hundred meters from here.
È a un chilometro da qui.	It's a kilometer from here.

QUIZ 13

1. *lì in Italia*	a. I expect to see him there.
2. *Mi aspetti qui.*	b. in there
3. *qui*	c. to the left
4. *a destra*	d. It's far.
5. *lì*	e. here
6. *È proprio qui.*	f. Wait for me here.
7. *Io spero di vederlo lì.*	g. straight ahead
8. *a sinistra*	h. to the right
9. *È lontano.*	i. there
10. *lì dentro*	j. Go there.
11. *È lì, da qualche parte.*	k. Go that way.
12. *È vicino.*	l. It's right here.
13. *Vada lì.*	m. over there in Italy
14. *Vada per quella strada.*	n. It's somewhere around there.
15. *sempre avanti*	o. It's near.

ANSWERS
1—m; 2—f; 3—e; 4—h; 5—i; 6—l; 7—a; 8—c; 9—d; 10—b; 11—n; 12—o; 13—j; 14—k; 15—g.

REVIEW QUIZ 2

1. _____ (this) *ragazzo*
   a. *questa*
   b. *questo*
   c. *queste*
2. *Dammi* _____ (those, *fem.*).
   a. *quelle*
   b. *queste*
   c. *questo*
3. *Ho* _____ (here) *i libri.*
   a. *lui*
   b. *qui*
   c. *come*

4. *Venga* _____ (here).
   a. *lei*
   b. *lì*
   c. *qui*

5. *Domani vado* _____ (there).
   a. *lì*
   b. *noi*
   c. *come*

6. _____ (Where) *sta?*
   a. *Là*
   b. *Dove*
   c. *Qui*

7. *È* _____ (far) *da qui?*
   a. *lontano*
   b. *quella*
   c. *lì*

8. *Roberto* _____ (and) *Giovanni sono fratelli.*
   a. *con*
   b. *e*
   c. *più*

9. *cinque* _____ (or) *sei giorni*
   a. *o*
   b. *e*
   c. *più*

10. *Desidero venire* _____ (but) *non posso.*
    a. *o*
    b. *ma*
    c. *fino*

ANSWERS

1—b; 2—a; 3—b; 4—c; 5—a; 6—b; 7—a; 8—b; 9—a; 10—b.

LESSON 14

A. I, You, He, etc. (Subject Pronouns)

The use of the subject pronouns is optional: "I speak" is just
parlo; "we speak," *parliamo;* etc. But the pronouns are used
for emphasis or clarity:

Io studio, tu ti diverti.	I study, you enjoy yourself.
Lui è inglese, lei è francese.	He is English; she is French.

SINGULAR

I, You, He, She

io	I
tu	you *(familiar)*
lui	he
lei	she
Lei	you *(polite)*
io parlo	I speak
tu parli	you speak *(familiar)*
lui parla	he speaks
lei parla	she speaks
Lei parla	you speak *(polite)*

PLURAL

We, You, They

noi	we
voi	you
loro	they
Loro	you *(formal)*
noi parliamo	we speak
voi parlate	you speak *(plural)*
loro parlano	they speak
Loro parlano	you speak *(formal)*

B. It's Me (I), You, He, etc.

Sono io.	It's I.
Sei tu.	It's you. *(familiar)*
È lui.	It's he.
È lei.	It's she.
Siamo noi.	It's we.
Siete voi.	It's you. *(plural)*
Sono loro.	It's they.

C. It and Them (Direct Object Pronouns)

	SINGULAR		PLURAL	
MASCULINE	**lo**	it	**li**	them
FEMININE	**la**	it	**le**	them

Ha il denaro?	Do you have the money *(polite)*
Sì ce l'ho.[1]	Yes I have it.
Ha la borsetta?	Do you have the handbag? *(polite)*
Sì, ce l'ho.[1]	Yes, I have it.
Ha visto Pietro e Giovanni?	Have you seen Peter and John?
Sì, io li ho visti.	Yes, I have seen them.
Ha visto Maria e Luisa?	Have you seen Mary and Louise?
Sì, io le ho viste.	Yes, I saw them.

Notice that the pronoun agrees in gender and number with the word it refers to. *Lo* and *la* elide; *li* and *le* do not. *Lo* is used when the reference is to an idea or a whole expression:

Lo capisco.	I understand it.

Lo, la, etc. usually come immediately before the verb, as in the case of other object pronouns. However, they may be added to the infinitive (which then drops its final *e*):

---

[1] *Lo* and *la* elide to *l'* before vowel sounds.

Lo voglio capire. =   I want to understand it.
Voglio capirlo.

D. WORD STUDY

banda	band
composizione	compostion
coscienza	conscience
decorazione	decoration
descrizione	description
missione	mission
numero	number
ottimista	optimist *(masc./fem.)*
regione	region

LESSON 15

A. MY, YOUR, HIS/HER, ETC. (POSSESSIVE ADJECTIVES)

mio, -a, -ei, -e	my
tuo, -a, -oi, -e	your *(fam.)*
suo, -a, -oi, -e	his, her, your *(polite)*
nostro, -a, -i, -e	our
vostro, -a, -i, -e	your *(pl.)*
loro	their, your *(formal pl.)*

In Italian the possessive adjective is always preceded by the definite article, except when it comes before members of the family in the singular. *Loro* is always preceded by the article.

tuo fratello	your brother
mia figlia	my sister
il loro figlio	their son

Study the following examples:

SINGULAR

il mio amico	my friend *(masc.)*
la mia amica[1]	my friend *(fem.)*
il tuo amico	your friend
il suo amico	his/her friend
il nostro amico	our friend
la nostra amica	our friend
il vostro amico	your friend
la vostra amica	your friend
il loro amico	their friend

PLURAL

i miei amici	my friends
i tuoi amici	your friends
i suoi amici	their friends
i nostri amici	our friends
le nostre amiche	our friends *(fem.)*
i vostri amici	your friends
le vostre amiche	your friends *(fem.)*
i loro amici	their friends

SINGULAR

il mio cappello	my hat
il tuo vestito	your dress/suit
il suo vestito	his/her dress/suit
il nostro amico	our friend
la nostra borsa	our bag
il vostro cavallo	your horse
la vostra penna	your pen

---

[1] Note that the possessive adjective agrees in gender with the noun that follows rather than with the subject: *la mia amica* = my (female) friend. The speaker may be male or female.

PLURAL

i miei cappelli	my hats
i tuoi vestiti	your clothes
i suoi vestiti	his/her clothes
i nostri amici	our friends
le nostre borse	our bags
i vostri cavalli	your horses
le vostre penne	your pens

B. IT'S MINE, YOURS, HIS, ETC. (POSSESSIVE PRONOUNS)

È mio, mia, etc.[1]	It's mine.
È tuo.	It's yours. *(fam.)*
È Suo.	It's yours. *(polite)*
È nostro.	It's ours.
È vostro.	It's yours.
È il loro.	It's theirs.
È il mio.	It's mine.
È il tuo.	It's yours.
È il Suo.	It's yours. *(polite)*
È il nostro.	It's ours.
È il vostro.	It's yours.
È il loro.	It's theirs.

Other examples:

i miei amici ed i tuoi	my friends and yours
Il suo libro è migliore del nostro.	His book is better than ours.

Generally the article is used with the possessive; however, in some cases it is omitted.

Di chi è questa lettera?	Whose is this letter?
È sua.	It's his.

[1] As with possessive adjectives, the gender of possessive pronouns depends on the noun they are replacing rather than the gender of the speaker.

C. To/For/About Me, You, Him, etc. (Prepositional Pronouns)

Notice the form of the pronoun when it comes after a preposition (see Section 32 in the Grammar Summary for more prepositions):

per me	for me
per te	for you
con lui	with him
a lei	to her
a te	for you
senza di noi	without us
con voi	with you
per loro	for them
di voi	of, about you

Io parlo di te.	I'm speaking about you.
Marco va senza di noi.	Mark is going without us.
Vuole andare con me.	He wants to go with me.
Lei parla di lui.	She is speaking about him.
Scrivono a voi.	They write to you.

D. Direct and Indirect Object Pronouns

1. Direct object pronouns take the place of the direct object in a sentence; they receive the action of the verb. In Lesson 14, Section C, *lo/la* and *li/le* (it and them) appeared; the following group of phrases shows all the direct object pronouns:

   a. He sees me, you, him, etc.

Lui mi vede.	He sees me.
Lui ti vede.	He sees you. *(familiar)*
Io lo vedo.	I see him.
Io la vedo.	I see her.
Io La vedo.	I see you. *(polite)*

Loro ci vedono.	They see us.
Noi vi vediamo.	We see you. *(fam. pl.)*
Noi li vediamo.	We see them. *(masc.)*
Noi le vediamo.	We see them. *(fem.)*

b. She buys it.

Maria lo compra.	Maria buys it.
	(a *masc. sing.* noun)
Maria la compra.	Maria buys it.
	(a *fem. sing.* noun)
Maria li compra.	Maria buys them.
	(a *masc. plur.* noun)
Maria le compra.	Maria buys them.
	(a *fem. plur.* noun)

2. Indirect object pronouns indicate the person to, for, or from whom any action occurs, and they are the ultimate recipients of the verb's action. (In English, you sometimes use "to" before the indirect object pronoun.) Study these phrases:

a. He tells me . . .

Lui mi dice . . .	He tells me . . .
Lui ti dice . . .	He tells you . . . *(fam. sing.)*
Lui gli dice . . .	He tells him . . .
Lui le dice . . .	He tells her . . .
Lui ci dice . . .	He tells us . . .
Lui vi dice . . .	He tells you . . .
Lui dice a loro . . .	He tells them . . .

b. I'm speaking to you.

Io Le parlo.	I'm speaking to you. *(polite)*
Lui ti parla.	He is speaking to you.
Lui Le parla.	He is speaking to you. *(polite)*

3. When there are two object pronouns in a sentence, the indirect precedes the direct, and both precede the conjugated verb[1]:

a. He gives it to me.

Lui me lo dà.	He gives it to me.
Lui te lo dà.	He gives it to you. *(fam. sing.)*
Lui glielo dà.	He gives it to him/her/you. *(polite)*
Lui ce lo dà.	He gives it to us.
Lui ve lo dà.	He gives it to you.
Lui lo dà a loro.	He gives it to them.

Notice the change in the form of some of the pronouns according to their position in the sentence. Remember that *loro* always follows the verb.

E. MYSELF, YOURSELF, HIMSELF, ETC. (REFLEXIVE PRONOUNS)

1. Notice the forms for "myself," "yourself," etc.: *mi, ti, si*, etc. Verbs that take these "reflexive pronouns" are called "reflexive" verbs.

lavarsi	to wash up, to wash oneself
Io mi lavo.	I wash myself. I get washed.
Tu ti lavi.	You wash yourself. You get washed.
Lui si lava.	He washes himself.
Lei si lava.	She washes herself./You wash yourself. *(polite)*
Noi ci laviamo.	We wash ourselves.
Voi vi lavate.	You wash yourselves.
Loro si lavano.	They wash themselves./You wash yourselves. *(formal)*

[1] See also Section 28 in the Grammar Summary.

Other examples:

Come si chiama?   What's your name? (How do
                                   you call yourself?)

Noi ci vediamo nello   We see ourselves in the mirror.
specchio.

2. Many verbs that are reflexive in Italian are not in
English:

Mi diverto.   I'm having a good time.
Mi siedo.   I sit down. I'm sitting down.
Mi alzo.   I get up. I'm getting up
                             (standing up).
Mi dimentico.   I forget.
Mi ricordo.   I remember.
Mi fermo.   I stop.
M'addormento.   I fall asleep.
Mi sbaglio.   I'm mistaken.

3. In Italian you don't say "I'm washing my hands," but
"I'm washing the hands"; not "Take your hat off," but
"Take off the hat":

Io mi lavo le mani.   I'm washing my hands.
Si tolga il cappello.   Take your hat off. *(polite)*
Lui si è rotto il braccio. He broke his arm.
Lei si è tagliato il dito. She cut her finger.
Mi sono fatto male alla I've hurt my hand.
mano.
Mi fa male la testa.   My head hurts. I have a
  Ho mal di testa.   headache.
Mi fa male lo stomaco. My stomach hurts. I have a
  Ho mal di stomaco.   stomachache.
Sto perdendo la pazienza. I'm losing my patience.

4. The reflexive forms are often used where we would
use the passive in English:

Qui si parla italiano.   Italian is spoken here.
Le porte si aprono alle   The doors open at eight.
    otto.

    The reflexive forms are also often used to translate our "one," "they," "people," etc.

Si dice che . . .   It's said that . . . People say
                           that . . . They say that . . .

Qui si mangia bene.   The food's good here. (One
                           eats well here.)

QUIZ 14

1. *Mi siedo.*	a. I get up.
2. *M'addormento.*	b. I stop.
3. *Mi diverto.*	c. I forget.
4. *Mi ricordo.*	d. I'm mistaken.
5. *Mi alzo.*	e. I wash myself.
6. *Mi lavo.*	f. I'm having a good time.
7. *Mi sbaglio.*	g. They sit down.
8. *Si siedono.*	h. I remember.
9. *Mi dimentico.*	i. I fall asleep.
10. *Mi fermo.*	j. I sit down.

ANSWERS

1—j; 2—i; 3—f; 4—h; 5—a; 6—e; 7—d; 8—g; 9—c; 10—b.

REVIEW QUIZ 3

1. *È* _____ (he).
    a. *lei*
    b. *lui*
    c. *io*
2. *Siamo* _____ (we).
    a. *loro*
    b. *tu*
    c. *noi*

3. *Io do il libro a* _____ (him).
    a. *lui*
    b. *voi*
    c. *loro*

4. *il* _____ (her) *vestito*
    a. *suo*
    b. *mio*
    c. *nostro*

5. *la* _____ (our) *carta*
    a. *nostro*
    b. *nostra*
    c. *tuo*

6. *Dove sono i* _____ (my) *libri?*
    a. *tuoi*
    b. *miei*
    c. *nostri*

7. *Il suo libro è migliore del* _____ (ours).
    a. *tuoi*
    b. *nostro*
    c. *suoi*

8. *Parliamo di* _____ (him).
    a. *te*
    b. *loro*
    c. *lui*

9. *Lui* _____ (to us) *lo dice.*
    a. *lui*
    b. *ce*
    c. *voi*

10. *Come si* _____ (call) *lei?*
    a. *lava*
    b. *chiama*
    c. *vede*

11. *Noi ci* _____ (wash).
    a. *lava*
    b. *lavano*
    c. *laviamo*

12. *Mi* _____ (to be mistaken).
    a. *sbaglio*
    b. *lavo*
    c. *giro*
13. *Mi* _____ (sit down).
    a. *vado*
    b. *ricordo*
    c. *siedo*
14. *Mi sono* _____ (hurt) *alla mano*.
    a. *sbagliato*
    b. *lavo*
    c. *fatto male*
15. *Qui* _____ (is spoken) *italiano*.
    a. *si parla*
    b. *si mangia*
    c. *si chiama*

ANSWERS

1—b; 2—c; 3—a; 4—a; 5—b; 6—b; 7—b; 8—c; 9—b;
10—b; 11—c; 12—a; 13—c; 14—c; 15—a.

LESSON 16

A. SOME ACTION PHRASES

Stia attento(-a)! Attenzione!	Watch out! *(polite)*
Faccia attenzione! Attento!	Be careful! Watch out! *(polite)*
Presto!	Fast! Hurry up!
Vada presto! Corra!	Go fast! Run! *(polite)*
Più presto!	Faster!
Non tanto di corsa.	Not so fast. (Don't run so much.)
Non molto in fretta. Non di corsa.	Not very fast. Not in a hurry.
Più piano. Senza fretta.	Slower. No hurry.
Meno in fretta.	Slower.

Vengo. Io vengo. Sto venendo.	I'm coming.
Vengo subito. Corro.	I'm coming right away.
Corra. Faccia presto.	Hurry up. *(polite)*
Non c'è fretta. Non corra.	There's no hurry. Don't rush (run). *(polite)*
Io ho fretta.	I'm in a hurry.
Non ho fretta.	I'm not in a hurry.
Un momento!	Just a minute! In a minute!
Al volo. Subito.	Right away.
Immediatamente.	Immediately.
Venga subito! Corra!	Come right away. *(polite)*
Presto.	Soon.
Immediatamente.	Immediately.
Più presto.	Sooner.
Più tardi.	Later.

B.   MAY I ASK . . . ?

Posso farLe una domanda?	May I ask you a question?
Posso domandarLe . . . ? Posso chiederLe . . . ?	May I ask (you) . . . ?
Puó dirmi . . . ?	Can you tell me . . . ?
Potrebbe dirmi . . . ?	Could you tell me . . . ?
Mi vuole dire . . . ?	Will you tell me . . . ?
Potrebbe dirmi . . . , per favore?	Could you please tell me . . . ?
Vuole farmi il piacere di dirmi . . . ?	Could you please tell me . . . ? *(formal)*
Che cosa vuol dire?	What do you mean?
Io voglio dire che . . .	I mean that . . .
Che cosa significa questo?	What does this mean?
Questo significa . . .	This means . . .

C.   WORD STUDY

destinazione	destination
diversione	diversion

liquido	liquid
obbligazione	obligation
occupazione	occupation
popolare	popular
solido	solid
teatro	theater

QUIZ 15

1. *Stia attento(-a)!* *Attenzione!*	a. Will you tell me . . . ?
2. *Io ho fretta.*	b. Right away.
3. *Io voglio dire che . . .*	c. Come right away!
4. *Presto.*	d. I'm coming!
5. *Che cosa significa questo?*	e. Watch out!
6. *Più tardi.*	f. Later.
7. *Mi vuole dire . . . ?*	g. I'm in a hurry.
8. *Vengo! Sto venendo!*	h. I want to say that . . .
9. *Venga subito! Corra!*	i. What does this mean?
10. *All'istante. Subito.*	j. Soon.

ANSWERS

1—e; 2—g; 3—h; 4—j; 5—i; 6—f; 7—a; 8—d; 9—c; 10—b.

LESSON 17

A. NUMBERS

uno	one
due	two
tre	three
quattro	four
cinque	five
sei	six

sette	seven
otto	eight
nove	nine
dieci	ten
undici	eleven
dodici	twelve
tredici	thirteen
quattordici	fourteen
quindici	fifteen
sedici	sixteen
diciassette	seventeen
diciotto	eighteen
diciannove	nineteen
venti	twenty
ventuno	twenty-one
ventidue	twenty-two
ventitrè	twenty-three
trenta	thirty
trentuno	thirty-one
trentadue	thirty-two
trentatrè	thirty-three
quaranta	forty
quarantuno	forty-one
quarantadue	forty-two
quarantatrè	forty-three
cinquanta	fifty
cinquantuno	fifty-one
cinquantadue	fifty-two
cinquantatrè	fifty-three
sessanta	sixty
sessantuno	sixty-one
sessantadue	sixty-two
sessantatrè	sixty-three
settanta	seventy

settantuno	seventy-one
settantadue	seventy-two
settantatrè	seventy-three
ottanta	eighty
ottantuno	eighty-one
ottantadue	eighty-two
ottantatrè	eighty-three
novanta	ninety
novantuno	ninety-one
novantadue	ninety-two
novantatrè	ninety-three
cento	hundred
centouno	a hundred and one
centodue	a hundred and two
centotrè	a hundred and three
mille	thousand
milledue	a thousand and two
milletrè	a thousand and three

B. MORE NUMBERS

centoventi	120
centoventidue	122
centotrenta	130
centoquaranta	140
centocinquanta	150
centosessanta	160
centosettanta	170
centosettantuno	171
centosettantotto	178
centottanta	180
centottantadue	182
centonovanta	190
centonovantotto	198
centonovantanove	199

duecento		200
trecentoventiquattro		324
ottocentosettantacinque		875

primo	*-a, -i, -e*	first
secondo	*-a, -i, -e*	second
terzo	*-a, -i, -e*	third
quarto	*-a, -i, -e*	fourth
quinto	*-a, -i, -e*	fifth
sesto	*-a, -i, -e*	sixth
settimo	*-a, -i, -e*	seventh
ottavo	*-a, -i, -e*	eighth
nono	*-a, -i, -e*	ninth
decimo	*-a, -i, -e*	tenth

due e due fanno quattro	two and two are four
due più due fanno quattro	two and two are four
quattro più due fanno sei	four and two are six
dieci meno due fanno otto	ten minus two is eight

C. WORD STUDY

amministrazione	administration
carattere	character
curioso	curious
tenda	curtain
dizionario	dictionary
grado	degree
ufficiale	official
piatto	plate

QUIZ 16

1. *mille*
2. *undici*
3. *cento*
4. *diciassette*

a. 1,002
b. 32
c. 102
d. 324

5. *trenta*		e.	11
6. *venti*		f.	1,000
7. *sessanta*		g.	60
8. *trecentoventiquattro*		h.	71
9. *trentadue*		i.	17
10. *centodue*		j.	875
11. *ottocentosettantacinque*		k.	83
12. *settantuno*		l.	93
13. *mille e due*		m.	20
14. *novantatrè*		n.	30
15. *ottantatrè*		o.	100

ANSWERS

1—f; 2—e; 3—o; 4—i; 5—n; 6—m; 7—g; 8—d; 9—b;
10—c; 11—j; 12—h; 13—a; 14—l; 15—k.

LESSON 18

A. How Much?

Quanto costa questo?	How much does this cost?
Costa un euro.	It costs one euro.
Quanto costa un chilo di caffè?	How much is a kilo of coffee?
Costa cinque euro.	It costs five euros.

B. It Costs . . .

Costa . . .	It costs . . .
Questo libro costa dieci euro.	This book costs ten euros.
Lui ha comprato un automobile per quindicimila euro.	He bought a car for fifteen thousand euros.

Il viaggio in treno da Roma a Milano costa cinquantacinque euro.	The trip by train from Rome to Milan costs fifty-five euros.
Ho risparmiato trecento euro per comprarmi un abito.	I've saved three hundred euros to buy a suit.
Lui ha guadagnato nel mese di giugno duemilaottocentotrenta-quattro euro.	He made 2,834 euros in the month of June.
Si vende solamente al chilo e costa un euro cinquanta.	It's sold only by the kilo and costs one euro fifty (cents).

C. My Address Is . . .

Io abito in Via Nazionale, al numero duecento cinquanta.	I live at 250 Nazionale Street.
Lei abita in Corso Italia numero trecento.	She lives at 300 Corso d'Italia.
Il negozio si trova in Viale Mazzini, al numero trecentoventisei.	The store is at 326 Mazzini Avenue.
Loro si sono trasferiti in Piazza Venezia, al numero novecento-ventuno.	They moved to 921 Venezia Square.

D. My Telephone Number Is . . .

Il mio numero di telefono è sei tre due otto otto tre tre.	My telephone number is 63-28-833.
Il loro numero di telefono è quattro zero otto sei zero due quattro.	Their telephone number is 40-86-024.
Non dimentichi il mio numero di telefono: otto sei cinque zero sei cinque sette.	Don't forget my telephone number: 86-50-657.

Centralinista, mi dia il numero quattro zero tre sei nove quattro sette.	Operator, may I have 40-36-947?
Il numero quattro zero tre sei nove quattro sette non risponde.	There's no answer at number 40-36-947.

E. THE NUMBER IS . . .

Il numero è . . .	The number is . . .
Il mio numero è . . .	My number is . . .
Il numero della mia camera è trenta.	My room number is 30.
Io abito nella camera numero trenta.	I live in room 30.
Il numero della mia casa è mille trecento ventidue.	My address (house number) is 1322.
Io abito al numero trecento trentadue del Viale Quinto, al quinto piano.	I live at 332 Fifth Avenue, on the fifth floor.

LESSON 19

A. WHAT'S TODAY?

Che giorno della settimana è oggi?	What day of the week is today?
È lunedì.	It's Monday.
È martedì.	It's Tuesday.
È mercoledì.	It's Wednesday.
È giovedì.	It's Thursday.
È venerdì.	It's Friday.
È sabato.	It's Saturday.
È domenica.	It's Sunday.

To say, "on Sunday . . ." etc. in Italian, simply state the day:

Arrivo sabato.	I arrive (on) Saturday.
Vada lunedì.	Go (on) Monday.

To express a habitual action, use the definite article with the day of the week:

Non lavoriamo il sabato.	We don't work on Saturdays.
Mangio tardi la domenica.	I eat late on Sundays.

The following expressions all mean "What's the date?":

Quanti ne abbiamo?	(How many days do we have?)
Qual è la data oggi?	(What is the date today?)
Che giorno è oggi?	(What day is today?)

The following expressions all mean "It's the 20th":

Siamo al venti.	(We're at the 20th.)
È il venti.	(It's the 20th.)
Ne abbiamo venti.	(We have twenty of them.)

On + days of the month is expressed by the masculine definite article + a cardinal number, except for the first of the month, which is *il primo:*

il primo luglio	on July 1
il cinque aprile	on April 5

Che giorno è oggi?	What's today's date?
È il primo maggio.	It's the 1st of May.
È l'undici aprile.	It's the 11th of April.
È il quattro luglio.	It's the 4th of July.
È il quindici settembre.	It's the 15th of September.
È il ventun giugno.	It's the 21st of June.
È il venticinque dicembre.	It's the 25th of December.
È il diciassette novembre.	It's the 17th of November.
È il tredici febbraio.	It's the 13th of February.
È il ventotto agosto.	It's the 28th of August.

B. SOME DATES

L'America fu scoperta nel millequattrocentonovantadue.	America was discovered in 1492.

"I Promessi Sposi" fu pubblicato nel milleottocentoventicinque.	"I Promessi Sposi" ("The Betrothed") was published in 1825.
Dante nacque nel mille-duecentosessantacinque, e morì nel milletrecentoventuno.	Dante was born in 1265, and died in 1321.
Noi siamo stati lì nel millenovecentottanta-quattro.	We were there in 1984.
Oggi è il ventidue febbraio millenovecento-novantanove.	Today is February 22, 1999.
Il suo compleanno è il quindici gennaio.	His birthday is January 15.
Nel dicianovesimo secolo . . .	In the 19th century . . .
Negli anni sessanta . . .	In the Sixties . . .

C. WORD STUDY

conclusione	conclusion
cemento	cement
contratto	contract
decisione	decision
persona	person
segnale	signal
stagione	season
stazione	station

QUIZ 17

1. *È lunedì.*
2. *Che giorno del mese è oggi?*
3. *il primo luglio*
4. *Che giorno è oggi?*

a. the 25th of June
b. the 28th of February
c. the 13th of August
d. in 1990

5. *l'undici aprile*	e. It's Monday.
6. *il ventotto febbraio*	f. What day of the month is it?
7. *il venticinque giugno*	g. date
8. *nel millenovecento novanta*	h. July first
9. *il tredici agosto*	i. the 11th of April
10. *data*	j. What's today's date?

ANSWERS

1—e; 2—f; 3—h; 4—j; 5—i; 6—b; 7—a; 8—d; 9—c; 10—g.

LESSON 20

A. WHAT TIME IS IT?

Che ora è?	What time is it?
È l'una.	It's 1:00 o'clock.
Sono le due.	It's 2:00.
Sono le tre.	It's 3:00.
Sono le quattro.	It's 4:00.
Sono le cinque.	It's 5:00.
Sono le sei.	It's 6:00.
Sono le sette.	It's 7:00.
Sono le otto.	It's 8:00.
Sono le nove.	It's 9:00.
Sono le dieci.	It's 10:00.
Sono le undici.	It's 11:00.
Sono le dodici.	It's 12:00 noon.
È mezzogiorno.	It's noon.
È mezzanotte.	It's midnight.
minuto	minute
ora	hour
Che ora è, per favore?	What time is it, please?

Ha l'ora, per favore?	Do you have the time, please?
Il mio orologio fa le cinque.	It's 5 o'clock by my watch. (My watch marks 5 o'clock.)
È l'una e cinque.	It's 1:05.
È l'una e dieci.	It's 1:10.
È l'una e quindici.	It's 1:15.
È l'una e un quarto.	It's 1:15.
È l'una e mezza.	It's 1:30.
È l'una e cinquanta.	It's 1:50.
Sono le due meno dieci.	It's 1:50. (two less ten)
Sono le tre e dieci.	It's 3:10. (three and ten)
Sono le sei e tre quarti.	It's 6:45. (six and three quarters)
Sono le due meno un quarto.	It's 1:45. (two less a quarter)
Non sono ancora le quattro.	It's not four yet.
A che ora parte il treno?	At what time does the train leave?
Alle nove in punto.	At 9 o'clock sharp.
Alle nove precise.	Exactly at 9 o'clock.
Alle nove circa.	About 9 o'clock.
Verso le nove.	Around 9 o'clock.

B. AT WHAT TIME?

A che ora?	At what time?
All'una.	At one o'clock.
Alle sette di mattina.	At 7 A.M.
Alle tre meno venti del pomeriggio.	At 2:40 P.M. (three minus twenty in the afternoon)
Alle quindici meno venti.	At 2:40 P.M. (fifteen hours less twenty minutes)
Alle sei di sera.	At 6 P.M.
Alle diciotto.	At 6 P.M. (At 18:00.)
Alle sei del pomeriggio.	At 6 P.M.

Notice that when you want to specify "A.M." or "P.M." in Italian, you add *di mattina* (in the morning), *del pomeriggio* (in the afternoon), *di sera* (in the evening), *di notte* (at night). In Italy, as in most European countries, the 24-hour clock (used by the military in the U.S.) is generally used for transportation schedules and theater times. From 1 A.M. to 12:00 noon, the time is the same as the 12-hour system. After noon, just keep counting, so that 1 P.M. is 13 hours, 2 P.M. is 14 hours, etc. Midnight, or 24 hours, is also expressed as 00:00.

C. IT'S TIME

È ora.	It's time.
È ora di farlo.	It's time to do it.
È ora di partire.	It's time to leave.
È ora di andare a casa.	It's time to go home.
Ho molto tempo.	I have a lot of time.
Non ho tempo.	I don't have any time.
Lui sta perdendo tempo.	He is wasting (losing)
Perde tempo.	time.
Lui viene di tanto in tanto.	He comes from time to time.

D. WORD STUDY

assoluto	absolute
aspetto	aspect
bar	bar
cambio	exchange
certo	certain
combinazione	combination
maniera	manner
pericolo	danger
rischio	risk

QUIZ 18

1. *È ora di farlo.*	a. He comes from time to time.
2. *Che ora è?*	b. It's 9:00.
3. *È l'una.*	c. At what time?
4. *Sono le tre.*	d. It's time to do it.
5. *Sono le nove.*	e. It's 2:00.
6. *È mezzanotte.*	f. It's 1:00.
7. *A che ora?*	g. I don't have any time.
8. *Non ho tempo.*	h. It's 2:40 P.M.
9. *È l'una e un quarto.*	i. It's noon.
10. *Sono le quattro.*	j. It's 3:00.
11. *Sono le due.*	k. It's 1:05.
12. *Lui viene di tanto in tanto.*	l. It's 4:00.
13. *È mezzogiorno.*	m. What time is it?
14. *È l'una e cinque.*	n. It's 1:15.
15. *Sono le tre meno venti del pomeriggio.*	o. It's midnight.

ANSWERS

1—d; 2—m; 3—f; 4—j; 5—b; 6—o; 7—c; 8—g; 9—n;
10—l; 11—e; 12—a; 13—i; 14—k; 15—h.

LESSON 21

A. YESTERDAY, TODAY, TOMORROW, ETC.

PASSATO	PRESENTE	FUTURO
ieri	**oggi**	**domani**
yesterday	today	tomorrow
ieri mattina	**stamattina**	**domani mattina**
yesterday morning	**(questa mattina)** this morning	**(domattina)** tomorrow morning

ieri sera	**stasera**	**domani sera**
last evening	**(questa sera)**	tomorrow
	this evening	evening

ieri notte	**questa notte**	**domani notte**
last night	**(stanotte)**	tomorrow
	tonight	night

B. Morning, Noon, Night, etc.

stamattina (questa mattina)	this morning
ieri mattina	yesterday morning
domani mattina	tomorrow morning
questo pomeriggio	this afternoon
ieri pomeriggio	yesterday afternoon
domani pomeriggio	tomorrow afternoon
stasera (questa sera)	this evening
ieri sera	yesterday evening
domani sera	tomorrow evening
questa notte (stanotte)	tonight
ieri notte	last night
domani notte	tomorrow night

C. This Week, Next Month, in a Little While, etc.

questa settimana	this week
la settimana scorsa	last week
la settimana entrante	next week
la settimana prossima	next week
fra due settimane	in two weeks
due settimane fa	two weeks ago
questo mese	this month
il mese scorso	last month
il mese entrante	next month
il mese che viene	the coming month

fra due mesi	in two months
due mesi fa	two months ago
quest'anno	this year
l'anno scorso	last year
l'anno prossimo	next year
l'anno che viene	the coming year
fra due anni	in two years
due anni fa	two years ago
Quanto tempo fa?	How long ago?
un momento fa	a moment ago
molto tempo fa	a long time ago
ora	now, for the time being
in questo momento preciso	at this very moment
da un momento all'altro	at any moment
per il momento	for the time being
in questo momento	at this moment
in breve tempo	in a short time
in poco tempo	in a little while
di tanto in tanto	from time to time
Quante volte?	How many times?
una volta	once
ogni volta	each time
due volte	twice
raramente	rarely
non spesso	not often
molte volte	many times, often
molto spesso	very often
a volte/qualche volta	sometimes
ogni tanto	once in a while
di tanto in tanto	now and then; from time to time
di mattina presto	early in the morning
al crepuscolo	in the evening (twilight)
al tramonto	at nightfall
il giorno seguente	the following day
il giorno dopo	the day after

fra due settimane	in two weeks
fra una settimana	in a week
domani alle otto	tomorrow at eight
mercoledì prossimo	next Wednesday
il lunedì della settimana scorsa	Monday of last week
il cinque di questo mese	the fifth of this month
il cinque del mese passato	the fifth of last month
all'inizio di marzo	at the beginning of March
alla fine del mese	at the end of the month
all'inizio dell'anno	in the early part of the year
verso la fine dell'anno	toward the end of the year
Avvenne otto anni fa.	It happened eight years ago.
È successo otto anni fa.	It happened eight years ago.

QUIZ 19

1. *ieri mattina*
2. *questa sera*
3. *domani sera*
4. *ieri notte*
5. *il mese entrante*
6. *ora*
7. *la settimana scorsa*
8. *l'anno scorso*
9. *oggi a mezzogiorno*

10. *in poco tempo*
11. *questa settimana*
12. *Avvenne otto anni fa.*
13. *verso la fine dell'anno*
14. *due mesi fa*
15. *verso la fine del mese*
16. *fra una settimana*
17. *di tanto in tanto*

a. last year
b. last night
c. today at noon
d. now
e. in two weeks
f. in a little while
g. yesterday morning
h. from time to time
i. It happened eight years ago.
j. this evening
k. sometimes
l. in a week
m. tomorrow evening
n. next month
o. last week
p. each time
q. about the end of the month

18. *a volte*   r. toward the end of the
                                           year
19. *fra due settimane*   s. this week
20. *ogni volta*   t. two months ago

ANSWERS

1—g; 2—j; 3—m; 4—b; 5—n; 6—d; 7—o; 8—a; 9—c;
10—f; 11—s; 12—i; 13—r; 14—t; 15—q; 16—l; 17—h;
18—k; 19—e; 20—p.

REVIEW QUIZ 4

1. *Compro un' automobile per* _____ (thirty thousand)
   euro.
   a. *tremila*
   b. *quattrocento*
   c. *trentamila*
2. *Il numero del suo telefono è* _____ (408-60-42).
   a. *sei, cinque, zero, sei, nove, sei, zero*
   b. *tre, sei, nove, due, zero, quattro, due*
   c. *quattro, zero, otto, sei, zero, quattro, due*
3. *Che* _____ (date) *abbiamo?*
   a. *giorno*
   b. *mese*
   c. *data*
4. *Che* _____ (day) *è oggi?*
   a. *mese*
   b. *giorno*
   c. *come*
5. *il* _____ (17) *dicembre*
   a. *dicisassette*
   b. *ventisette*
   c. *cinque*
6. *È* _____ (1:10).
   a. *l'una e cinque*
   b. *l'una e dieci*
   c. *l'una e un quarto*

7. *Sono le* _____ (7).
   a. *sette*
   b. *nove*
   c. *sei*

8. *È* _____ (12 noon).
   a. *mezzanotte*
   b. *mezzogiorno*
   c. *undici*

9. *Sono le* _____ (2:40).
   a. *le quattro meno un quarto*
   b. *le tre meno venti*
   c. *le due meno un quarto*

10. _____ (yesterday) *mattina*
    a. *oggi*
    b. *ieri*
    c. *e*

11. *la* _____ (week) *scorsa*
    a. *settimana*
    b. *notte*
    c. *domani*

12. *fra due* _____ (months)
    a. *settimane*
    b. *giorni*
    c. *mesi*

13. *Sono due* _____ (years).
    a. *mesi*
    b. *anni*
    c. *giorni*

14. *il* _____ (Wednesday) *della settimana entrante*
    a. *lunedì*
    b. *venerdì*
    c. *mercoledì*

15. *alla* _____ (end) *dell'anno*
    a. *fine*
    b. *inizio*
    c. *primo*

ANSWERS
1—c; 2—c; 3—c; 4—b; 5—a; 6—b; 7—a; 8—b; 9—b;
10—b; 11—a; 12—c; 13—b; 14—c; 15—a.

LESSON 22

A. Not, Nothing, Never, No One

The word for "not," *non*, comes before the verb:

io non vedo	I don't see
tu non vedi	you don't see
Non vedo nulla.	I see nothing. I don't see anything.
Non vado mai.	I never go.
Non vengono.	They are not coming.
Non vedo niente.	I see nothing. I don't see anything.
Non vado mai via.	I never go away.
Nessuno viene.	No one is coming.
Non viene nessuno.	
Sì, signore.	Yes, sir.
No, signora.	No, ma'am.
Dice di sì.	He (She) says yes.
Dice di no.	He (She) says no.
Credo di sì.	I think so.
Non è bene.	It's not good.
Non è male.	It's not bad.
Non è quello.	It's not that.
Non è qui.	He's (She's) not here.
Non è troppo.	It's not too much.
Non è abbastanza.	It's not enough.
È abbastanza.	It's enough.

Non tanto in fretta.	Not so fast.
Non così in fretta.	
Non tanto spesso.	Not so often.
Non così spesso.	
Non è nulla. È nulla.	It's nothing.
Questo è nulla. Ciò è nulla.	That's nothing.
Non è molto importante.	It's not very important.
Non ho tempo.	I have no time.
Non so nè come nè quando.	I don't know how or when.
Non so dove.	I don't know where.
Non so nulla.	I don't know anything.
Non so niente.	
Non ne so nulla.	I know nothing about it.
Non so nulla di ciò.	
Non voglio nulla.	I don't want anything.
Non desidero nulla.	
Non importa.	It doesn't matter. It's not
Non fa niente.	important.
Non me ne importa.	I don't care. It makes no
	difference to me.
Non me ne importa niente.	I don't care at all.
Non me ne importa affatto.	It doesn't make the slightest
	difference to me.
Non lo dica.	Don't say it. *(polite)*
Non ho nulla da dire.	I have nothing to say.
Non lo dirò mai.	I'll never say it.
Non è successo nulla.	Nothing happened.
Non ho niente da fare.	I have nothing to do.
Non lo vedo mai.	I never see him.
Non l'ho mai visto prima.	I've never seen him before.
Non l'ho mai visto.	I've never seen him.
Non viene mai.	He (She) never comes.
Non è mai venuto.	He has never come.
Non vado mai.	I never go.
Non andrò mai.	I'll never go.

B. NEITHER . . . NOR . . .

Non ho detto una parola, nè una sillaba.
I haven't said a word, nor a syllable.

Non posso andare nè voglio andare.
I can't go, nor do I want to go.

Nè . . . nè . . .
Neither . . . nor . . .

Nè più nè meno.
Just so (neither more nor less).

Nè l'uno nè l'altro.
Neither the one nor the other. (Neither one.)

Nè questo nè quello.
Neither this nor that.

Nè molto nè poco.
Neither (too) much nor (too) little.

Nè bene nè male.
So-so. Neither good nor bad.

Non ho nè tempo nè denaro.
I have neither the time nor the money.

Non sa nè leggere nè scrivere.
He (She) can neither read nor write.

Non ho nè sigarette nè fiammiferi.
I have neither cigarettes nor matches.

C. WORD STUDY

antagonista	enemy
avanzamento	advance
banco	bank
capitolo	chapter
contento	content
delizioso	delicious
energia	energy
errore	mistake
frutto	fruit
ricco	rich

QUIZ 20

1. *Non vedo.*
2. *Non è nulla.*
3. *Non lo dirò mai.*
4. *Non vado mai via.*
5. *Lui non vede Giovanni.*
6. *Non credo.*
7. *Non tanto in fretta.*
8. *Non so nulla.*
9. *Non vedo nulla.*
10. *Io non l' ho mai visto.*
11. *Non me ne importa.*
12. *Non è successo nulla.*
13. *Lui non viene mai.*
14. *Non è male.*
15. *Non andrò mai.*
16. *Non è qui.*
17. *Nessuno viene.*
18. *Nè questo nè quello.*
19. *Non me lo dica.*
20. *Non ho tempo.*

a. Neither this nor that.
b. I have no time.
c. Don't tell it to me.
d. Nothing happened.
e. I don't see.
f. I don't know anything.
g. I've never seen him.
h. He doesn't see John.
i. I'll never say it.
j. He never comes.
k. I see nothing.
l. I'll never go.
m. It's nothing.
n. He's (She's) not here.
o. I don't think so.
p. It's not bad.
q. I don't care.
r. Not so fast.
s. I never go away.
t. No one is coming.

1—e; 2—m; 3—i; 4—s; 5—h; 6—o; 7—r; 8—f; 9—k;
10—g; 11—q; 12—d; 13—j; 14—p; 15—l; 16—n; 17—t;
18—a; 19—c; 20—b.

LESSON 23

A. Isn't It? Aren't They? Don't You?

È vero?
Is it? (Is it true?)

Non è vero?
Isn't it? (Isn't it true?)

L'italiano è facile, non è vero?
Italian is easy, isn't it?

La gente qui è molto gentile, vero?
The people here are very nice, aren't they?

Lei non ha una matita, vero?
You don't have a pencil, do you?

Lei conosce questo posto, non è vero?
You know this place, don't you?

Lei conosce il signor Rossi, vero?
You know Mr. Rossi, don't you?

Lei ha un cucchiaio e un tovagliolo, vero?
You have a spoon and a napkin, don't you?

Lei non è qui da molto tempo, vero?
You haven't been here very long, have you?

Lei verrà, vero?
You will come, won't you?

Fa freddo, vero?
It's cold, isn't it?

È molto carino! Non è carino?
It's very cute! It's cute, isn't it?

Va bene, vero?
It's all right, isn't it?

B. SOME, ANY, A FEW

Ha (Lei) dei soldi?
Do you have any money?

Sì, ne ho.
Yes, I have some.

No, non ne ho.
No, I don't have any.

Ha (lui) dei soldi?
Does he have any money?

Ne ha.
He has some.

Non ne ha affatto.
He doesn't have any at all.

Ha ancora dei soldi? Le sono rimasti dei soldi?
Do you still have money? Do you have any money left?

Me ne sono rimasti un po'.
I have some left. (Some remains to me.)

Quanti libri ha?
How many books do you have?

Ne ho pochi.
I have few.

Desidera un po' di frutta?
Do you want some fruit?

Me ne dia un po'.
Give me some. *(polite)*

Ce ne dia un po'.
Give us some. *(polite)*

Ne dia un po' a lui.
Give him some. *(polite)*

alcuni dei miei amici
some of my friends

C. LIKE, AS, HOW

come
like, as, how

come me
like me

come quello
like that

come questo
like this

come noi
like us

come gli altri
like the others

Questo non è come quello.
This one isn't like that one.

È così.
That's how it is.

Come desidera.
As you wish. *(polite)*

È come a casa propria.
It's like (being at) home.

Lui non è come suo padre.
He's not like his father.

Com' è?
What's it like?

È bianco come la neve.
It's as white as snow.

Come piove!
What rain! (How it's raining!)

Come? Cosa dice?
What? What did you say? What do you mean?

Perchè no? Come no?
Why not?

QUIZ 21

1. *Come desidera.*	a. He's not like his father.
2. *come gli altri*	b. What? What did you say?
3. *come questo*	c. Give him some. *(polite)*
4. *Ha (Lei) del denaro?*	d. Why not?
5. *alcuni dei miei amici*	e. It's all right, isn't it?
6. *Non è come suo padre.*	f. As you wish. *(polite)*
7. *Come?*	g. Do you have any money?
8. *Ne dia un po' a lui.*	h. like the others
9. *Perchè no?*	i. like this
10. *Va bene, non è vero?*	j. some of my friends

ANSWERS

1—f; 2—h; 3—i; 4—g; 5—j; 6—a; 7—b; 8—c; 9—d;
10—e.

LESSON 24

A. HAVE YOU TWO MET?

Buon dì.
Hello.

Salve.
Hi. *(fam.)*

Conosce il mio amico?
Do you know my friend? *(pol.)*

(È un) piacere.
(It's) a pleasure.

Credo che ci siamo già conosciuti.
I believe we've met before.

Non credo di aver avuto il piacere.
I don't believe I've had the pleasure.

Non ho avuto il piacere (di conoscerLa).
I haven't had the pleasure (of meeting you).

Credo che vi conoscete già, non è vero?
I believe you already know each other, don't you?

Credo che ci conosciamo.
I think we know each other.

Ho già avuto il piacere di conoscerlo.
I've already had the pleasure of meeting him.

Mi permetta di presentarLa al mio amico Antonio Marchi.
Allow me to introduce you to my friend Antonio Marchi.

B. HELLO, HOW ARE YOU?

Buon giorno.
Good morning. Good day.

Come sta?
How do you do? How are you? *(pol.)*

Ciao.
Hi. Bye. *(fam.)*

Come stai?
How are you? *(fam.)*

Non c'è male. E Lei?
So-so. And you?

E tu?
And you?

E come sta Lei?
And how are you?

E come stai tu?
And how are you?

Che c'è di nuovo?
What's new?

Niente di nuovo.
Nothing much. (Nothing new.)

Nulla di importante.
Nothing much. (Nothing important.)

C'è niente di nuovo?
(Isn't there) anything new?

Non c'è niente di nuovo.
There's nothing new.

Com'è mai non ci si vede?
Where have you been? *(fam.)*

Com'è che non La si vede mai?
Where have you been? (How is it that no one ever sees you?)
(pol.)

Sono stato molto occupato(-*a*) in questi giorni.
I've been very busy these days.

Mi telefoni qualche volta.
Give me a call sometime. *(polite)*

Le telefonerò uno di questi giorni.
I'll call you one of these days. *(pol.)*

Ti telefonerò uno di questi giorni.
I'll call you one of these days. *(fam.)*

Perchè non viene a trovarci a casa?
Why don't you come to see us (to our house)? *(polite)*

Verrò a trovarvi la settimana prossima.
I'll come to visit you next week.

Non dimentichi la Sua promessa.
Don't forget your promise. *(pol.)*

Non dimenticare la tua promessa.
Don't forget your promise. *(fam.)*

Alla prossima settimana, allora.
Until next week, then.

Arrivederci alla settimana prossima.
See you next week. (Until next week.)

C. WORD STUDY

angolo	angle
causa	cause
distanza	distance
effetto	effect

industria　　　　　　industry
opinione　　　　　　 opinion
oscuro　　　　　　　 obscure
proprietario　　　　　proprietor

LESSON 25

A. GLAD TO HAVE MET YOU

Sono lieto(-*a*) di averLa conosciuta.
Glad to have met you.

Molto liet*o*(-a).
Glad (happy) to have met you.

Spero di vederLa presto.
Hope to see you again soon.

Lo spero anch'io.
I hope so, too.

Ecco il mio indirizzo e il mio numero di telefono.
Here's my address and telephone number.

Ha il mio indirizzo?
Do you have my address? *(polite)*

No, me lo dia.
No, let me have it. *(polite)*

Eccolo qui.
Here it is.

Molte grazie.
Thanks a lot.

Si fa tardi.
It's getting late.

È ora di rientrare.
It's time to go back.

Partiamo domani.
We're leaving tomorrow.

Quando posso telefonarLe?
When can I call you *(polite)*?

Di mattina.
In the morning.

La chiamerò dopodomani.
I'll call you *(polite)* the day after tomorrow.

Aspetterò la Sua chiamata.
I'll be expecting your *(polite)* call.

B. GOOD-BYE

ArrivederLa.
Good-bye. *(pol.)*.

Arrivederci.
Good-bye. *(fam.)*

Ciao.
Bye. *(fam.)*

A più tardi.
See you later.

A dopo.
See you later. *(fam.)*

Arrivederci ad un'altra volta.
So long, see you again. (Until another time.)

Alla prossima.
Until next time.

A domani.
See you tomorrow. (Till tomorrow.)

A sabato.
See you Saturday. (Till Saturday.)

QUIZ 22

1. *Spero di vederLa presto.*
2. *ArrivederLa.*
3. *Sono lieto(-a) di averLa conosciuta.*
4. *Ha il mio indirizzo?*
5. *Eccolo qui.*
6. *Di mattina.*
7. *A domani.*
8. *Aspetterò la Sua chiamata.*
9. *Molte grazie.*
10. *A sabato.*

a. Do you have my address?
b. See you tomorrow.
c. I'll be expecting your call.
d. Till Saturday.
e. In the morning.
f. Glad to have met you.
g. Thanks a lot.
h. Hope to see you soon.
i. Here it is.
j. Good-bye.

ANSWERS

1—h; 2—j; 3—f; 4—a; 5—i; 6—e; 7—b; 8—c; 9—g; 10—d.

C. VISITING SOMEONE

Abita qui il signor Giovanni Rossi?
Does Mr. John Rossi live here?

Sì, abita qui.
Yes, he does. (He lives here.)

A che piano?
On what floor?

Terzo piano, a sinistra.
Third floor, on the left.

È in casa il signor Rossi?
Is Mr. Rossi at home?

No, signore. È uscito.
No, sir. He's gone out.

A che ora sarà di ritorno?
A che ora ritornerà?
At what time will he be back?

Non so dirLe.
I couldn't say. (I don't know how to tell you.)

Desidera lasciar detto qualche cosa?
Do you want to leave him a message?

Gli lascerò un biglietto . . .
I'll leave him a note . . .

Se mi può dare una matita e un foglio di carta.
If you can, give me a pencil and a piece of paper.

Ritornerò questa sera.
I'll come back tonight.

Ritornerò domani.
I'll come back tomorrow.

Ritornerò un altro giorno.
I'll come back another day.

Gli dica di telefonarmi, per favore.
Please tell him to call me.

Sarò in casa tutto il giorno.
I'll be at home all day.

QUIZ 23

1. *terzo piano, a sinistra*
2. *Ritornerò più tardi.*
3. *Abita qui il signor Giovanni Rossi?*
4. *È uscito.*
5. *A che ora ritornerà?*
6. *È in casa?*
7. *Che piano?*
8. *Gli dica di telefonarmi.*
9. *Sarò in casa tutto il giorno.*
10. *Abita qui.*

a. I'll be at home all day.
b. Is he at home?
c. At what time will he be back?
d. He lives here.
e. What floor?
f. Tell him to call me.
g. He's gone out.
h. Does Mr. John Rossi live here?
i. third floor, on the left
j. I'll come back later.

ANSWERS

1—i; 2—j; 3—h; 4—g; 5—c; 6—b; 7—e; 8—f; 9—a; 10—d.

LESSON 26

A. PLEASE

The most common ways of saying "please" are *per favore,* *per piacere,* or *mi faccia il favore,* which means literally "would you do me the favor of," and is reserved for formal settings or written correspondence.

Porti questo, per piacere.
Please carry this.

Entrino, per favore.
Please come in. (speaking to several people)

Per piacere, venga qui.
Please come here.

Per favore, mi faccia vedere i suoi documenti.
Please let me see your papers.

Per piacere, vuole chiamare un tassì?
Per piacere, vuole chiamare un taxi?
Will you please call a taxi?

Mi faccia il favore di venire.
Please come. (Do me the favor of coming.)

B. OTHER POLITE EXPRESSIONS

1. **Mi scusi. Mi perdoni.**
   Excuse me. Pardon me.
   Scusi il ritardo.
   Excuse my lateness.

2. **Per cortesia.**
   Please.

Per cortesia, il Suo biglietto.
Your ticket, please.
Per cortesia, sieda qui.
Please sit here.

3. **La prego.**
Please. (I pray you.)
La prego di farlo al più presto possibile.
Please do it as soon as possible.
La prego, puo dirmi dov'è la biblioteca?
Can you please tell me where the library is?

4. **Mi dispiace. Mi spiace. Mi scusi.**
I'm sorry.
Scusami. Chiedo scusa.
I apologize.
Perdonami, per favore. (per piacere, per cortesia)
Please forgive me.

5. *Desidero,* or *desidererei,* means "I would like to."

Desidera sedere qui?	Would you like to sit here?
Desidererei andare ma non posso.	I'd like to go, but I can't.

C. WORD STUDY

ambizione	ambition
brillante	brilliant
capitale	capital
contratto	contract
democrazia	democracy
dipartimento	department
monumento	monument
ostacolo	obstacle
recente	recent

QUIZ 24

1. *Desidera sedere qui?*	a. Excuse my lateness.
2. *Per favore, venga qui.*	b. Excuse me. Pardon me.
3. *Per favore, vuole chiamare un tassì?*	c. Please come here.
4. *Scusi il mio ritardo.*	d. Please carry this.
5. *Mi scusi. Mi perdoni.*	e. Please tell me where the library is.
6. *Per favore, entrino.*	f. Your ticket, please.
7. *Per favore, può dirmi dov' è la stazione?*	g. Will you please call a taxi?
8. *Per piacere, porti questo.*	h. Please come in.
9. *Per favore, il Suo biglietto.*	i. Can you please tell me where the station is?
10. *Per favore, mi dica dov' è la biblioteca.*	j. Would you like to sit here?

ANSWERS

1—j; 2—c; 3—g; 4—a; 5—b; 6—h; 7—i; 8—d; 9—f; 10—e.

REVIEW QUIZ 5

1. *È in* _____ (home, house) *il signor Rossi?*
   a. *appartamento*
   b. *ora*
   c. *casa*
2. *Desidera lasciare un* _____ (note)?
   a. *matita*
   b. *biglietto*
   c. *carta*
3. _____ (Excuse) *il mio rítardo.*
   a. *La prego*
   b. *Scusi*
   c. *Faccia*

4. _____ (Hope to) *vederLa presto.*
    a. *Desidero*
    b. *Spero di*
    c. *Sarò*

5. _____ (Please) *lo faccia al più presto possibile.*
    a. *Servire*
    b. *Mi scusi*
    c. *Per piacere*

6. *Ha la faccia bianca* _____ (as) *la neve.*
    a. *cui*
    b. *come*
    c. *questo*

7. _____ (I would like), *ma non posso.*
    a. *Io desidererei*
    b. *Ho*
    c. *Desidera*

8. _____ (Why) *non lo ha detto?*
    a. *Chi*
    b. *Perchè*
    c. *Di chi*

ANSWERS

1—c; 2—b; 3—b; 4—b; 5—c; 6—b; 7—a; 8—b.

LESSON 27

A. WHO? WHAT? WHEN? ETC.

1. *Chi?* = Who?

Chi è?	Who is he (she)?
Non so chi è.	I don't know who he (she) is.
Chi sono?	Who are they?
Chi lo ha detto?	Who said it?
Chi l' ha detto?	Who said so?
Chi l' ha fatto?	Who did it?

Di chi è questa matita?	Whose pencil is this?
Per chi è questo?	Who is this for?
Chi desidera vedere?	Whom do you wish to see?
A chi desidera parlare?	To whom do you wish to speak?
Chi lo sa?	Who knows (it)?
Di chi è questo?	Whose is this?

2. *Che? Che cosa?* = What?

Che cosa è questo?	What's this?
Che cosa è quello?	What's that?
Che cosa succede?	What's the matter? What's up?
Che c'è?	What's the matter? What's up?
Che è successo?	What happened?
Che c'è di nuovo?	What's new?
Cosa pensa? Che cosa pensa?	What do you think?
Cosa sono?	What are they?
Che cosa ha?	What do you have?
Cosa Le succede?	What's the matter with you?
Che ora è?	What time is it?
Che cosa dice?	What are you saying?
Che cosa ha detto?	What did you say?
Di che cosa sta parlando?	What are you talking about?
Di che si tratta?	What is it about?
Che cosa vuole?	What do you want?
Cosa posso fare per Lei?	What can I do for you?
Desidera?	What would you like?
I signori desiderano?	What would you like? *(pol. pl.)*

3. *Perchè?* = Why?

Perchè così?	Why so?
Perchè no?	Why not?
Perchè dice questo?	Why do you say that?
Perchè tanta fretta?	Why are you in such a hurry? Why the hurry?

Perchè l' ha fatto?   Why did you do it? *(polite)*
Perchè non viene?   Why don't you come?

4. *Come?* = How?

Come si dice questo in   How do you say this in
   italiano? ` Italian?
Come si chiama?   What is your name? (How do
                               you call yourself?) *(pol.)*
Come ti chiami?   What is your name? *(fam.)*
Come si scrive questo?   How is this spelled
                               (written)?

5. *Quanto?* = How much?

Quanto denaro desidera?   How much money do
                               you want?
Quanti libri ci sono?   How many books are there?
Quanto è distante   How far is it from
   Napoli da Firenze?   Naples to Florence?

6. *Quale?* = What? Which?

Qual'è il suo nome?   What is his name?
Quale desidera?   Which (one) do you want?
Quale desidera, questo o   Which (one) do you want, this
   quello?   one or that one?
Quale di queste matite è   Which one of these pencils is
   la Sua?   yours?
Quale di queste due strade   Which of these two roads
   porta a Siena?   leads to Siena?
Qual'è il suo indìrizzo?   What's his address?

7. *Dove?* = Where?

Dov'è il Suo amico?   Where is your friend?
Dove vive (lui)?   Where does he live?
Dove và (lei)?   Where is she going?

8. *Quando?* = When?

Quando verrà Suo fratello?	When will your brother come?
Quando è successo?	When did it happen?
Quando parte?	When are you going (leaving)?
Non so quando.	I don't know when.
Fino a quando?	Until when?
Per quanto tempo?	For how long?
Non so fino a quando.	I don't know how long. (I don't know until when.)
Quando? Fra quanto tempo?	When?
Quando Lei vuole.	When you wish.
Da quando?	Since when?
Com'è avvenuto?	How did it happen?
Quando è accaduto?	When did it happen?
Da quando è qui?	How long have you been here? (*polite*)

QUIZ 25

1. *Come si chiama?*
2. *Quanti libri ci sono?*
3. *Come si dice questo in italiano?*
4. *Che cosa dice?*
5. *Quando è successo?*
6. *Da quando?*
7. *Chi lo sa?*
8. *Perchè no?*
9. *Dove abita (lui)?*
10. *Come si scrive questo?*

a. When did it happen?
b. Since when?
c. Who knows?
d. Where does he live?
e. What's your name?
f. What are you saying?
g. Why not?
h. How do you write this?
i. How many books are there?
j. How do you say this in Italian?

1—e; 2—i; 3—j; 4—f; 5—a; 6—b; 7—c; 8—g; 9—d; 10—h.

B. What a Pity! What a Surprise!

Che peccato!	What a pity!
Che vergogna!	What a shame!
Che disgrazia!	How unfortunate! (What a misfortune!)
Che orrore!	How awful!
Che fortuna!	What luck! How lucky!
Che sorpresa!	What a surprise!
Com'è carino!	How cute (he/it is)!
Com'è grazioso! Com'è bello!	How beautiful!

REVIEW QUIZ 6

1. *Non vedo* _____ (nothing).
   a. *nessuno*
   b. *nulla*
   c. *mai*

2. *Non viene* _____ (nobody).
   a. *nessuno*
   b. *no*
   c. *mai*

3. *Non sa leggere* _____ (nor) *scrivere.*
   a. *no*
   b. *mai*
   c. *nè*

4. *L'italiano è facile,* _____ (isn't it)?
   a. *non è vero*
   b. *è vero*
   c. *no*

5. *Me ne dia* _____ (a little).
   a. *nulla*
   b. *un po'*
   c. *qualcosa*

6. *Desidera* _____ (some) *di frutta?*
   a. *alcuni*
   b. *pochi*
   c. *un po'*

7. *Non è* _____ (like) *suo padre.*
   a. *come*
   b. *è*
   c. *li altri*

8. *È stato molto* _____ (busy) *in questi giorni.*
   a. *sempre*
   b. *occupato*
   c. *nuovo*

9. *Si* _____ (know) *loro?*
   a. *conosciuti*
   b. *conoscono*
   c. *conoscerla*

10. *Con chi ho il piacere di* _____ (speak)?
    a. *parlare*
    b. *avere*
    c. *conoscere*

11. *Ecco il mio* _____ (address) *ed il mio numero di telefono.*
    a. *giorno*
    b. *biglietto*
    c. *indirizzo*

12. *Ci vedremo uno di questi* _____ (days).
    a. *giorni*
    b. *molto*
    c. *settimana*

13. *Lei ha la* _____ (mine).
    a. *molto*
    b. *mia*
    c. *giorno*

14. _____ (What) *dice?*
    a. *Come*
    b. *Quando*
    c. *Che*

15. _____ (Why) *è andata via?*
    a. *Che cosa*
    b. *Perchè*
    c. *Quanto*

16. _____ (How) *si dice questo in italiano?*
    a. *Come*
    b. *Quando*
    c. *Nessuno*

17. _____ (How much) *denaro desidera?*
    a. *A chi*
    b. *Quanto*
    c. *Di chi*

18. _____ (Who) *ha il suo vino?*
    a. *Chi*
    b. *Di chi*
    c. *Quale*

19. _____ (Where is) *il suo amico?*
    a. *Dov'è*
    b. *Come*
    c. *Chi*

20. _____ (When) *verrà suo fratello?*
    a. *Chi*
    b. *Quale*
    c. *Quando*

ANSWERS

1—b; 2—a; 3—c; 4—a; 5—b; 6—c; 7—a; 8—b; 9—b; 10—a; 11—c; 12—a; 13—b; 14—c; 15—b; 16—a; 17—b; 18—a; 19—a; 20—c.

LESSON 28

A. IT'S GOOD, IT'S WONDERFUL

Buono(-a).	Good. *(masc., fem.)*
È buono.	It's good.
Molto buono.	Very good.
È molto buono.	It's very good.
È eccellente.	It's excellent.
È stupendo.	It's wonderful.
È magnifico.	It's excellent. It's wonderful.
È ammirabile.	It's excellent. It's admirable.
È perfetto.	It's perfect.
È fantastico.	It's great. *(fem.)*
È forte.	It's cool.
È di moda.	It's in (trendy).
È giusto.	It's correct.
Non c'è male.	It's not bad.
Va bene?	Is it all right?
Molto bene.	Very well.
Molto buono.	Very good.
È bella.	She's beautiful.
È bellissima.	She's very beautiful.
È molto carina.	She's very pretty, cute.
È attraente.	She's charming.
È bello.	He's handsome.
È galante.	He's charming.
È carino.	He's cute.
È bravo.	He's a great guy.
È brava.	She's a good sport.
È molto alla mano.	She (He) is a good sport.

B. IT'S NOT GOOD, IT'S WORTHLESS

Non è buono(-a).	It's not good. It's no good. *(masc., fem.)*

Non è molto buono.	It's not very good.
Quello non è buono.	That's not good.
Questo non è giusto.	This isn't right.
Questo non è corretto.	This isn't correct. This is wrong.
È male.	It's bad.
È molto male.	It's very bad.
È pessimo.	That's very bad. That's the worst.
È fatto malissimo.	It is done very badly.
È veramente cattivo.	It's really (truly) bad.
Non mi interessa.	I don't care. It doesn't interest me.
Questo non vale niente.	That's worthless.
Non serve a nulla.	It's worthless. It's good for nothing.
Uffa! Che noia!	What a drag!
È orribile!	It's horrible!
È pessimo!	It's the worst!
Che schifo!	How disgusting!

QUIZ 26

1. *Va bene.*
2. *Molto bene.*
3. *È eccellente.*
4. *Non c'è male.*
5. *È male.*
6. *Che peccato!*
7. *È molto carina.*
8. *Non serve a nulla.*
9. *Che disgrazia!*
10. *È stupendo.*

a. It's excellent.
b. She's very pretty.
c. That's worthless.
d. What a pity!
e. How unfortunate!
f. It's wonderful!
g. It's all right.
h. That's bad.
i. Very well.
j. It's not bad.

ANSWERS
1—g; 2—i; 3—a; 4—j; 5—h; 6—d; 7—b; 8—c; 9—e; 10—f.

LESSON 29

A. I LIKE IT

Mi piace . . .	I like . . . (It pleases me . . .)
Mi piace molto.	I like it (him, her) a lot.
Mi piace moltissimo.	I like it (him, her) very much.
Mi piace quello.	I like that.
Lei mi piace.	I like her.
Mi piacciono molto.	I like them a lot.
La musica mi piace molto.	I love music.
Le piace?	Do you like it?
Non Le piace?	Don't you like it?
Le piace la frutta?	Do you like fruit?
Si, la frutta mi piace.	Yes, I like fruit.
Non mi piace.	I don't like it.
Non mi piace molto.	I don't like it very much.
No, la frutta non mi piace.	No, I don't like fruit.
Le piace il cioccolato?	Do you like chocolate?
Le piace l'America?	Do you like America?
Le piace la cucina italiana?	Do you like Italian food?
Le piace l'Italia?	Do you like Italy?
Le è piaciuta l'Italia?	Did you like Italy?
L'Italia mi è piaciuta.	I liked Italy.
Crede che la casa gli piacerà?	Do you think they'll like the house?
Vi piace la mia camera?	How do you all like my room?
Non mi piace.	I don't like it.
Non mi piace molto.	I don't like it very much.
Se Le piace.	If you like it.
Quando Le piace.	Whenever you like.
Quando desidera.	Whenever you want.

Notice that the Italian for "I like fruit" is *mi piace la frutta* (fruit is pleasing to me). That is, the word which is the object in English is the subject in Italian. "I like the United States" is *mi piacciono gli Stati Uniti* (the United States are pleasing to me). Here the verb is plural because the subject *(gli Stati Uniti)* is plural.

B. I Don't Care

Non m'importa.	I don't care.
Non me ne importa niente.	I couldn't care less.
Non me ne importa un fico secco.	I don't give a damn.
Non m'importa affatto.	I don't care at all.
Chi se ne importa?	Who cares?
Non importa.	It doesn't make any difference.

C. I Had a Good Time

Mi sono divertito(a).	I had a good time
Ci siamo divertiti un sacco!	We had a blast!
Non mi sono divertito(a).	I didn't have a good time.
È stata una perdita di tempo. È stato uno spreco di tempo.	It was a waste of time.
Divertiti! Buon divertimento!	Have a good time! *(singular)*
Divertitevi! Buon divertimento!	Have a good time! *(plural)*

QUIZ 27

1. *Le piace la cucina italiana?*
2. *Le piace?*
3. *Mi piace molto.*
4. *Le piace la frutta?*

a. I don't like it very much.
b. Do you like my room?
c. Do you like Italy?
d. If you like.

5. *Quando Le piace.*   e. Don't you like it?
6. *Le piace l'Italia?*   f. I like it very much.
7. *Non le piace?*   g. Do you like it?
8. *Se le piace.*   h. Whenever you like.
9. *Non mi piace molto.*   i. Do you like Italian food?
10. *Le piace la mia camera?*   j. Do you like fruit?

ANSWERS

1—i; 2—g; 3—f; 4—j; 5—h; 6—c; 7—e; 8—d; 9—a;
10—b.

LESSON 30

A. In, To, From, etc. (Prepositions)

Abito in Italia.	I live in Italy.
Sono stato(-a) a Roma.	I've been in Rome.
Vado a Roma.	I'm going to Rome.
Vengo da Roma.	I come from Rome.
Parto per Roma.	I'm leaving for Rome.
Lui va verso Roma.	He's going toward Rome.
Sono andato(-a) fino a Roma.	I went as far as Rome.
Vado in Europa.	I am going to Europe.

1. *A* = To, In

a destra	to the right
a sinistra	to the left
due a due	two by two
poco a poco	little by little
a piedi	on foot
a mano	by hand
a mezzogiorno	at noon
a mezzanotte	at midnight
Si sono seduti a tavola.	They sat down at the table.

all' italiana	in the Italian manner
A domani.	Until tomorrow.
A presto.	See you soon. (Until soon.)
A più tardi.	See you later. (Until later.)
Arrivederci.	Good-bye.
Alla prossima volta.	Until next time.

2. *Con* = With

Io sono andato(-a) con Giovanni.	I went with John.
Lui lo ha scritto con una matita.	He wrote it with a pencil.

3. *Di* = Of, From

È di mio fratello.	It's my brother's.
Io sono di Roma.	I am from Rome.
È fatto di legno.	It's made of wood.
di giorno	by day, in the daytime
di nuovo	again (of new)

4. *In* = In

Ho vissuto in Italia per vari anni.	I lived in Italy for several years.
Il treno partirà in orario.	The train will leave on time.
Venga in salotto.	Come into the parlor. *(polite)*
in quella direzione	in that direction

5. *Fino a* = Up to, Until

fino a Milano	up to (as far as) Milano
Io sono salito(-a) fino al quinto piano.	I walked up to the fifth floor.

6. *Verso* = Toward, Around (Approximately)

Lei camminava verso il parco.	She was walking toward (in the direction of) the park.

Ha cominciato a piovere verso mezzanotte.	It started to rain around midnight.

7. *Da* = From, Since

da Napoli a Capri	from Naples to Capri
da quando l'ho visto	since I saw him; since the time when I saw him

8. *Per* = For, Through, In place of

L'ho comprato per un dollaro.	I bought it for a dollar.
Gli ho dato un dollaro per questo.	I gave him a dollar for this.
Lui mi ha dato il suo libro per il mio.	He exchanged books with me. (He gave me his book for mine.)
Noi siamo passati per Roma.	We passed through Rome.
Il treno passa per Roma.	The train passes through Rome.
Lui è entrato per la porta.	He came in through the door.
Io vado per Lei.	I'll go for (in place of) you.
Io sarò in viaggio per due anni.	I'll be away traveling for two years.

9. *Sopra* = On, Above, Over

sopra la tavola	above the table
Lei aveva un cappotto sopra le spalle.	She had a coat on her back.

10. *Su* = On, On top of

La tovaglia è sulla tavola.	The tablecloth is on the table.
Ha un velo sui capelli.	She has a veil on her hair.

B. OTHER PREPOSITIONAL EXPRESSIONS

a causa di	on account of
alla fine	eventually
disposto(a) a farlo	in favor of doing it
di conseguenza	consequently, as a result
di notte	at night
invece di questo	instead of this
in generale	in general
nella mattina	in the morning, during the morning
nel pomeriggio	during the afternoon, in the afternoon
Perchè?	Why? What is the reason?
per ora	for the time being
per esempio	for example
per quanto riguarda	in regard to
per quella ragione	for that reason
Lui ha camminato per la strada.	He walked along the street.
Per amor di Dio!	For goodness' sake! For heaven's sake!
qui intorno	around here

C. WORD STUDY

ballo	ball
biglietto	ticket
formaggio	cheese
civile	civil
educazione	education, manners
efficiente	efficient
logico	logical
tavola	table

QUIZ 28

1. *a mezzogiorno*	a. on foot
2. *poco a poco*	b. one by one
3. *a destra*	c. I come from Rome.
4. *all'italiana*	d. It's made of wood.
5. *con*	e. by day
6. *a piedi*	f. again
7. *Vengo da Roma.*	g. on the table
8. *È fatto di legno.*	h. to the right
9. *per quanto riguarda*	i. in that direction
10. *di nuovo*	j. little by little
11. *in quella direzione*	k. until tomorrow
12. *di giorno*	l. at noon
13. *a sinistra*	m. For heaven's sake!
14. *uno a uno*	n. in the Italian manner
15. *fino a Milano*	o. with
16. *Partirò fra due giorni.*	p. instead of
17. *sulla tavola*	q. to the left
18. *a domani*	r. in regard to
19. *invece di*	s. as far as Milano
20. *Per amor di Dio!*	t. I'm leaving in two days.

ANSWERS

1—l; 2—j; 3—h; 4—n; 5—o; 6—a; 7—c; 8—d; 9—r; 10—f; 11—i; 12—e; 13—q; 14—b; 15—s; 16—t; 17—g; 18—k; 19—p; 20—m.

QUIZ 29

1. *per esempio*	a. I gave him a dollar for this.
2. *Il treno passa per Roma.*	b. I'll be traveling for two years.
3. *Siamo passati per Roma.*	c. completely
4. *per ora*	d. for that reason

5. *L'ho comprato per un dollaro.*	e. around here
6. *per quella ragione*	f. For goodness' sake!
7. *Io sarò in viaggio per due anni.*	g. at last
8. *completamente*	h. for example
9. *Io gli ho dato un dollaro per questo.*	i. I am not in favor of
10. *Per amor di Dio!*	j. for the time being
11. *alla fine*	k. I bought it for a dollar.
12. *Lui è entrato per la porta.*	l. The train passes through Rome.
13. *qui intorno*	m. I take this instead of that.
14. *non sono disposto(-a)*	n. He came in through the door.
15. *Prendo questo invece di quello.*	o. We passed through Rome.

ANSWERS

1—h; 2—l; 3—o; 4—j; 5—k; 6—d; 7—b; 8—c; 9—a;
10—f; 11—g; 12—n; 13—e; 14—i; 15—m.

LESSON 31

A. ON THE ROAD

Scusi. Perdoni.
Excuse me. Pardon me. *(polite)*

Mi perdoni.
Pardon me. *(polite)*

Mi scusi.
Excuse me. *(polite)*

Qual'è il nome di questo paese?
What is the name of this town?

Quanto siamo distanti da Roma?
How far are we from Rome?

Quanti chilometri ci sono da qui a Roma?
How many kilometers are there from here to Rome?

È dieci chilometri da qui.
It's ten kilometers from here.

È venti chilometri da qui.
It's twenty kilometers from here.

Come arrivo a Roma da qui?
How do I get to Rome from here?

Segua questa strada.
Follow this road. *(polite)*

Come si arriva a questo posto?
How do you get to this place?

È molto lontano?
Is it very far?

Qual'è la via più breve per andare a Torino?
What's the shortest way to get to Turin?

Quale strada devo prendere?
Which road should I take?

Dov'è il parcheggio?
Where is the parking lot?

B. WALKING AROUND

Può dirmi come posso arrivare a questo indirizzo?
Can you tell me how I can get to this address?

Può dirmi come posso arrivare a questo posto?
Can you tell me how I can get to this place?

Come si chiama questa strada?
What is the name of this street?

Puo indicarmi dov'è Via Veneto?
Can you direct me to Veneto Street?

Dov'è questo indirizzo?
Where is this address?

È qui vicino Via Barberini?
Is Barberini Street near here?

Penso di essermi smarrito(-a).
I think I'm lost.

Dov'è un telefono pubblico?
Where is there a public phone?

Può dirmi dov'è questa strada?
Can you tell me where this street is?

Dov'è Via Rossini?
Where is Rossini Street?

È lontano da qui?
Is it far from here?

È vicino?
Is it near?

È la terza strada a destra.
It's the third street on the right.

Vada per questa strada.
Go this way. *(polite)*

Vada avanti diritto.
Go straight ahead. *(polite)*

Vada fino all'angolo e volti a sinistra.
Go to the corner and turn left. *(polite)*

Prenda la prima strada a sinistra.
Take the first street to the left. *(polite)*

Volti a destra.
Turn right. *(polite)*

Dov'è la Questura?
Where is the Police Station?

Dov'è il Municipio?
Where is City Hall?

C. TAKING A BUS, TRAIN, TAXI, OR SUBWAY

Dov'è la fermata dell'autobus?
Where is the bus stop?

A quale fermata scendo?
At what stop do I get off?

Si ferma qui l'autobus?
Does the bus stop here?

Dove scendo?
Where do I get off?

Dov'è la stazione ferroviaria?
Where is the railroad station?

Quanto è lontana da qui la stazione?
How far is the station from here?

Siamo ancora lontani dalla stazione?
Are we still far from the station?

Dove si prende il treno per Roma?
Where do you get the train for Rome?

Da quale binario parte il treno per Roma?
From which track does the train for Rome leave?

A quale binario arriva il treno di Roma?
At which track does the Rome train arrive?

Dov'è l'ufficio informazioni?
Where is the information office?

Vuole darmi per favore un orario ferroviario?
Could you please give me a timetable?

Qual'è il treno per Roma?
Which is the train for Rome?

È questo il treno per Roma?
Is this the train for Rome?

Dove si prende il treno per Roma?
Where do you get the train for Rome?

Al binario due.
On track two.

Quando parte il treno per Roma?
When does the train for Rome leave?

Il treno è appena partito.
The train just left.

Il treno sta per partire.
The train is about to leave.

Quando parte il prossimo treno?
When does the next train leave?

Dov'è lo sportello dei biglietti?
Where is the ticket window?

Mi dia un biglietto di andata per Roma.
Give me a one-way ticket to Rome. *(polite)*

Un biglietto di andata e ritorno per Roma, per favore.
A round-trip ticket to Rome, please.

Di prima o di seconda classe?
First or second class?

Prima classe.
First class.

Quanto costa?
How much does it cost?

Tre euro.
Three euros.

Quanto tempo ci vuole per arrivare?
How long does it take to get there?

Un po' più di un'ora.
A little more than an hour.

È occupato questo posto?
Is this seat taken?

Posso mettere la mia valigia qui?
May I put my suitcase here?

Che stazione è questa?
What station is this?

Per quanto tempo ci fermiamo qui?
How long do we stop here?

Devo cambiare treno qui?
Do I change trains here?

Questo treno si ferma a Roma?
Does this train stop in Rome?

Tassì! *(Taxi!)*
Taxi!

È libero?
Are you free (unoccupied)?

Mi porti a questo indirizzo.
Take me to this address. *(polite)*

Quanto Le devo?
How much do I owe you?

Si ferma qui il tram?
Does the streetcar stop here?

A che fermata devo scendere?
At what stop do I get off?

Dov'è la stazione della metropolitana più vicina?
Where is the nearest subway station?

QUIZ 30

1. *Qual'è la via più breve per andare a ... ?*
2. *Dove posso telefonare?*
3. *Dov'è questa strada?*
4. *Mi porti a questo indirizzo.*
5. *Quanto è lontana la stazione?*
6. *Posso usare il Suo telefono?*
7. *Può indicarmi dov'è via ... ?*
8. *A quale fermata devo scendere?*
9. *Come si arriva a questo posto?*
10. *Si ferma qui l'autobus?*

a. How far is the station?
b. How do you get to this place?
c. Can you direct me to ... Street?
d. Does the bus stop here?
e. At which stop do I get off?
f. Where can I make a phone call?
g. Where is this street?
h. What's the shortest way to get to ... ?
i. Take me to this address.
j. May I use your phone?

ANSWERS
1—h; 2—f; 3—g; 4—i; 5—a; 6—j; 7—c; 8—e; 9—b; 10—d.

LESSON 32

A. WRITING AND MAILING LETTERS

Vorrei scrivere una lettera.
I'd like to write a letter.

Mi può dare un po' di carta?
Could you let me have (give me) some paper? *(polite)*

Qui c'è carta e una penna.
Here is some paper and a pen.

Ha una matita?
Do you have a pencil?

Ha una penna?
Do you have a pen?

Ha un foglio di carta?
Do you have a piece (leaf) of paper?

Ha una busta?
Do you have an envelope?

Ha un francobollo?
Do you have a stamp?

Dove posso comprare un francobollo?
Where can I buy a stamp?

Ha un francobollo per posta aerea?
Do you have an airmail stamp?

Vado all'ufficio postale.
I'm going to the post office.

Dov'è l'ufficio postale?
Where is the post office?

Vorrei imbucare questa lettera.
I'd like to mail this letter.

Quanti francobolli occorrono per questa lettera?
How many stamps do I need on this letter?

Ho bisogno di un francobollo per posta aerea.
I need an airmail stamp.

Ecco dei francobolli.
Here are some stamps.

Un francobollo per espresso, per favore.
A special delivery stamp, please.

Dov'è la cassetta delle lettere?
Dov'è la buca delle lettere?
Where is the mailbox?

Dov'è la cassetta postale più vicina?
Where is the nearest mailbox?

All'angolo.
On the corner.

Dov'è un telefono pubblico?
Where is the public telephone office?

È nell'ufficio postale.
It's in the post office.

B. FAXES AND E-MAIL

Devo spedire un facsìmile.
I have to send a fax.

Vorrei mandare un facsìmile.
I'd like to send a fax.

Quanto costa un facsìmile per Roma?
How much is a fax to Rome?

Da dove posso spedire un facsìmile?
From where can I fax?

Devo mandare un e-mail.
I have to send an e-mail message.

Posso collegarmi con internet?
Can I get on the Internet?

Avete un sito web?
Do you have a website?

Dov'è il computer?
Where is the computer?

C. TELEPHONING

C'è un telefono?
Is there a phone here?

Dove posso telefonare?
Where can I make a phonecall?

Dov'è il telefono?
Where is the telephone?

Dov'è la cabina telefonica?
Where is the phone booth?

Nell'atrio dell'albergo.
In the hotel lobby.

Posso usare il Suo telefono?
May I use your phone?

Sicuro! Si accomodi!
Of course! Go ahead! *(polite)*

Posso fare una chiamata interurbana?
Can I make a long distance call?

Quanto costa una telefonata per Roma?
How much is a phone call to Rome?

Posso avere il numero otto, sette, cinque, otto, due, quattro, tre?
May I have 87-58-243?

Aspetti un momento.
Hold on a minute. *(polite)*

La linea è occupata.
The line is busy.

Centralino, Lei mi ha dato il numero sbagliato.
Operator, you gave me the wrong number.

Non risponde.
There is no answer.

Posso parlare con il signor Ferri?
May I speak to Mr. Ferri?

In persona.
Speaking. (In person.)

Questo è il signor Villanova che parla.
This is Mr. Villanova speaking.

Parlo con il signor Ferri?
Am I speaking with Mr. Ferri?

Sono io.
Speaking. (It is I.)

Con chi parlo?
Who is this? (With whom am I speaking?)

Con il signor Ferri.
With Mr. Ferri.

D. WORD STUDY

computer (m.)	computer
portatile (m.)	laptop/portable computer
stampante	printer
schermo	screen
telefono cellulare; telefonino	cellular phone
segreteria telefonica	answering machine
posta vocale	voice mail
lasciare un messaggio	to leave a message
e-mail; posta elettronica	e-mail

QUIZ 31

1. *Dove posso comprare un francobollo?*
2. *La linea è occupata.*
3. *Sono io.*

a. Speaking.

b. Can I make a long distance call?

c. On the corner.

4. *Ha una busta?*	d. There is no answer.
5. *Posso fare una chiamata interurbana?*	e. Where can I buy a stamp?
6. *All' angolo.*	f. the wrong number
7. *Non risponde.*	g. I'd like to send a fax.
8. *Aspetti un momento.*	h. Do you have an envelope?
9. *il numero sbagliato*	i. Hold on a minute.
10. *Vorrei mandare un facsìmile.*	j. The line is busy.

ANSWERS

1—e; 2—j; 3—a; 4—h; 5—b; 6—c; 7—d; 8—i; 9—f; 10—g.

LESSON 33

A. WHAT'S YOUR NAME?

Come si chiama?
What's your name? *(pol.)*

Come ti chiami?
What's your name? *(fam.)*

Mi chiamo Giovanni Ferri.
My name is John Ferri.

Come si chiama *(lei)?*
What's her name?

Si chiama Maria Ferrari.
Her name is Maria Ferrari.

Come si chiamano?
What are their names?

Lui si chiama Giuseppe Riva e lei Anna Martini.
His name is Joseph Riva and her name is Anna Martini.

Qual'è il suo nome?
What's his (her) first name?

Il suo nome è Carlo.
His first name is Charles.

Qual'è il suo cognome?
What is his (her) last name?

Il suo cognome è Peretti.
His (her) last name is Peretti.

B.   WHERE ARE YOU FROM?

Di dov'è Lei?
Where are you from? *(pol.)*

Di dove sei *(tu)?*
Where are you from? *(fam.)*

Io sono di Roma.
I'm from Rome.

Dov'è nato (nata)?
Where were you born?

Sono nato (nata) a Roma.
I was born in Rome.

C. How Old Are You?

Quanti anni ha?
How old are you?

Ho ventiquattro anni.
I'm twenty-four.

Compirò ventiquattro anni a settembre.
I'll be twenty-four in September.

Sono nato il diciannove agosto millenovecentosessanta.
I was born August 19, 1960.

Quando è il Suo compleanno?
When is your birthday?

Il mio compleanno è fra due settimane, il ventitrè gennaio.
My birthday is in two weeks, January 23.

D. Professions

Qual è il Suo mestiere?
What do you do?

Sono artista.
I'm an artist.

Cosa fa Suo padre?
What does your father do?

Cosa fa Sua madre?
What does your mother do?

È avvocato. (È avvocatessa.)
He's (she's) a lawyer.

È architetto.
He's (she's) an architect.

È insegnante.
He's (she's) a teacher.

È professore d'università. (È professoressa d'università.)
He's (she's) a university professor.

È dottore. (È dottoressa.)
He's (she's) a doctor.

È uomo d'affari.
He's a businessman.

È una donna d'affari.
She's a businesswoman.

È agricoltore. (È agricoltrice.)
He's (she's) a farmer.

È un funzionario dello Stato.
He's (she's) a government worker.

È operaio. (È operaia.)
He's (she's) a worker.

Lavora in una fabbrica di automobili.
He (she) works in an automobile factory.

E. FAMILY MATTERS

Ha parenti qui?
Do you have any relatives here?

Quanti fratelli ha?
How many brothers do you have?

Ho due fratelli.
I have two brothers.

Il maggiore ha ventidue anni.
The older one is twenty-two.

Studia all'Università.
He is at the University.

Il minore ha quindici anni.
The younger one is fifteen.

Lui frequenta l'ultimo anno del liceo.
He's in his last year of high school.

Quante sorelle ha?
How many sisters do you have?

Ho una sorella.
I have one sister.

Ha nove anni.
She's nine.

Frequenta la scuola elementare.
She goes to grammar (elementary) school.

Vive qui tutta la Sua famiglia?
Does your whole family live here?

Tutta la mia famiglia, meno i miei nonni.
My whole family, except my grandparents.

Loro vivono in una villa di campagna vicino a Firenze.
They live in a country home near Florence.

È imparentato(*a*) con il signor Villanova?
Are you related to Mr. Villanova?

È mio zio.
He's my uncle.

È mio cugino.
He's my cousin.

È imparentato(*a*) con la signora Rossi?
Are you related to Mrs. Rossi?

È mia zia.
She's my aunt.

È mia cugina.
She's my cousin.

F. WORD STUDY

ansioso	anxious
consolato	consulate
differente	different
difficile	difficult
dottore	doctor
festa	feast
futuro	future
lingua	language
visita	visit

QUIZ 32

1. *Ho una sorella.*
2. *Di dov'è Lei?*
3. *Quanti anni ha Lei?*

a. What is his (her) first name?
b. I'm twenty-four.
c. Where are you from?

4. *Qual' è il suo nome?*	d. What are their names?
5. *È mia zia.*	e. She's my aunt.
6. *È insegnante.*	f. I have one sister.
7. *Come si chiamano?*	g. Are you related to Mr. Villanova?
8. *Sono nato(-a) a Roma.*	h. How old are you?
9. *Ho venti quattro anni.*	i. I was born in Rome.
10. *È imparentato(-a) con il signor Villanova?*	j. He's (she's) a teacher.

ANSWERS

1—f; 2—c; 3—h; 4—a; 5—e; 6—j; 7—d; 8—i; 9—b; 10—g.

LESSON 34

A. SHOPPING

1. **Quanto costa questo?**
   How much is this?

2. **Trenta euro.**
   Thirty euros.

3. **È piuttosto caro.**
   That's rather expensive.

   Non ha niente di più economico?
   Don't you have anything cheaper?

4. **Dello stesso modello?**
   In the same style?

5. **Lo stesso modello o qualche cosa di simile.**
   The same style or something similar.

6. **C'è questo.**
There's this.

7. **Non ha nient'altro da farmi vedere?**
Don't you have anything else you could show me?

8. **Meno caro?**
Less expensive?

9. **Se è possibile.**
If (it's) possible.

10. **Forse Le piace questo?**
Perhaps you like this?

11. **Dipende dal prezzo.**
That depends on the price.

12. **Questo costa diciassette euro.**
This one is seventeen euros.

13. **Mi piace più dell'altro.**
I like it better than the other one.

14. **È più economico.**
It's more affordable.

15. **Com'è questo? È più economico o più caro?**
How about this? Is it cheaper or more expensive?

16. **È più caro.**
It's more expensive.

17. **Non ha altro assortimento?**
Don't you have anything else in stock?

18. **Spero di ricevere presto nuovi modelli.**
I'm hoping to receive some new styles soon.

19. **Fra quanto?**
How soon?

20. **Da un giorno all'altro.**
Any day now.

Può ripassare verso la fine della settimana?
Can you drop in toward the end of the week?

21. **Lo farò . . . Quanto costano questi?**
I'll do that . . . What's the price of these?

22. **Due euro al paio.**
Two euros a pair.

23. **Me ne dia una dozzina.**
Let me have a dozen. *(polite)*

24. **Vuole portarli con sè?**
Will you take them with you? Will you take them yourself?

25. **Preferisco che me li mandi a casa.**
I'd rather have you send them to my house.

26. **L'indirizzo è sempre lo stesso?**
Is the address still the same?

27. **È lo stesso.**
It's the same.

28. **ArrivederLa.**
Good-bye.

NOTES

3. *È piuttosto caro* = That's rather expensive. *Molto caro* = very expensive. *Economico,* or *a buon mercato* = cheap. *Più economico* = cheaper. *Molto economico* = very cheap.

5. *Qualche cosa di simile* = something (of) similar.

7. *Da farmi vedere* = To let me see. You can also use *mostrarmi.*

19. *Fra quanto?* Idiomatic expression for "How soon?" It can also be expressed by *Fra quanto tempo?* (In how much time?)

20. *Da un giorno all'altro* = from one day to the other.

21. *Lo farò.* (I will do that.) Future of the verb *fare.*

23. *Me ne dia una dozzina.* (Give me a dozen of them.) *Dia* is the polite imperative of *dare.*

24. *Con se* = with yourself.
    Mandi: subjunctive of *mandare.*

28. *ArrivederLa* is used instead of *arrivederci* because the speaker is using the polite mode of address.

QUIZ 33

1. *È abbstanza* _____ (expensive).
    a. *costa*
    b. *questo*
    c. *caro*

2. *Ha nulla di più* _____ (cheap)?
   a. *qualità*
   b. *prezzo*
   c. *economico*

3. *Della* _____ (same) *qualità.*
   a. *qualche cosa*
   b. *stessa*
   c. *più*

4. _____ (Less) *caro.*
   a. *Più*
   b. *Meno*
   c. *Stesso*

5. *Mi piace* _____ (more) *dell'altro.*
   a. *come*
   b. *più*
   c. *vale*

6. *Non* _____ (have) *maggiore assortimento?*
   a. *ha*
   b. *caro*
   c. *altro*

7. *Spero* _____ (receive) *notizie.*
   a. *scelta*
   b. *tranquillo*
   c. *ricevere*

8. *A* _____ (when)?
   a. *assortimento*
   b. *caro*
   c. *quando*

9. *Allo stesso* _____ (address)?
   a. *indirizzo*
   b. *domicilio*
   c. *spedire*

ANSWERS
1—c; 2—c; 3—b; 4—b; 5—b; 6—a; 7—c; 8—c; 9—a.

LESSON 35

A. Breakfast in a Restaurant

1. P[1]: **Hai fame?**
   Are you hungry? (Do you have an appetite?)

2. Sig: **Sì, ho fame.**
   I certainly am.

3. P: **Cameriere! Cameriere!**
   Waiter! Waiter!

4. C: **Cosa desidera?**
   What would you like?

5. P: **Vorremmo fare colazione.**
   We'd like to have breakfast.

6. Sig: **Cosa ci può servire?**
   What can you serve us?

7. C: **Caffelatte, tè con limone o con latte, cioccolata ...**
   Coffee with milk, tea with lemon or with milk, hot chocolate ...

8. Sig: **Con che lo servite?**
   What do you serve with it?

9. C: **Con panini, paste, biscotti ...**
   Rolls, pastry, cookies ...

---

[1] "P" represents Mr. Paoli. "Sig" stands for *Signora* (his wife), and "C" for *Cameriere* (Waiter).

10. Sig: **C'è del burro?**
    Is there any butter?

11. C: **Sì, signora.**
    Yes, madam.

12. Sig: **Mi porta una tazza di caffè con latte, per piacere.**
    Bring me a cup of coffee with milk. *(polite)*

13. P: **Anche a me. E mi porti pure due uova fritte.**
    The same for me. And bring me also two fried eggs. *(polite)*

14. Sig: **Cameriere, mi porta un tovagliolo per favore ?**
    Waiter, would you please bring me a napkin? *(polite)*

15. P: **Per me, una forchetta.**
    And a fork for me.

16. Sig: **Per favore ci porta ancora un pò di zucchero.**
    Please bring us a little more sugar. *(polite)*

17. P: **E poi ci porti il conto . . . Ecco qui . . . tenga il resto.**
    And then let's have a check . . . Here you are . . . keep the change. *(polite)*

18. C: **Molte grazie, signore.**
    Thank you, sir.

NOTES

Breakfast is called *la prima colazione* or simply *colazione*. *Il pranzo* = lunch. *La cena* = dinner.

1. The subject pronoun is generally not used when the meaning of the sentence is obvious.

2. *Ho fame* = I have hunger.

4. *Che* is omitted. The sentence is really *Che cosa desidera?*

5. *Vorremmo*, conditional of *volere* (because it is a polite form).

9. *Panini* = rolls. *Panino imbottito* = sandwich (stuffed roll).

10. *Ha del burro?* = Have you of the butter? *del (di il contraction) burro*

13. *Un uovo* = an egg. *Uova* = eggs. (Note the irregular plural.) *Uova con pancetta* = bacon and eggs. *Uova alla cocca* = soft-boiled eggs ("in the shell"). *Uova sode* = hard-boiled eggs. *Uova strapazzate* = scrambled eggs.

14. *Tenga:* imperative of *tenere* (polite form). *Il resto* = the rest, the change (as a tip). *Spiccioli* = change, small money.

QUIZ 34

1. _____ (We would like) *fare colazione.*
   a. *Vorremmo*
   b. *Mangiare*
   c. *Appetito*
2. _____ (Is there) *del burro?*
   a. *Servire*
   b. *C'è*
   c. *Potrebbe?*
3. *Mi dia lo* _____ (same).
   a. *molto*
   b. *stesso*
   c. *spero*

4. *Chi va a* _____ (eat)?
   a. *servire*
   b. *poco*
   c. *mangiare*
5. *Io mangio molto* _____ (little).
   a. *vado*
   b. *questo*
   c. *poco*
6. *Per favore* _____ (bring me) *un tovagliolo.*
   a. *costume*
   b. *mi porti*
   c. *dirà*
7. _____ (Then) *ci porti il conto.*
   a. *Favore*
   b. *Forchetta*
   c. *Poi*

ANSWERS

1—a; 2—b; 3—b; 4—c; 5—c; 6—b; 7—c.

B. A SAMPLE MENU

LISTA	MENU
Antipasto	Hors d'oeuvres
Minestrone	Vegetable soup
Passato di piselli	Pea soup
Frittata al prosciutto	Ham omelet
Pollo arrosto (pollo alla diavola)	Roast chicken (devil-style chicken)
Abbacchio (alla romana)	Roast lamb (Roman style)
Bistecca con patate fritte	Steak with French fried potatoes
Insalata verde con pomodori	Green salad with tomatoes
Formaggio e frutta	Cheese and fruit
Caffè	Coffee

LESSON 36

A. APARTMENT HUNTING

1. **Sono venuta a vedere l'appartamento.**
   I've come to see the apartment.

2. **Quale? Quale dei due?**
   Which one? Which of the two?

3. **Quello che è da affittare.**
   The one that is for rent.

4. **Ce ne sono due.**
   There are two.

5. **Me li può descrivere?**
   Can you describe them?

6. **Quello al quinto piano non è ammobiliato.**
   The one on the fifth floor is unfurnished.

7. **E quell'altro?**
   And the other one?

8. **L'altro al secondo piano è ammobiliato.**
   The one of the second floor is furnished.

9. **Quante camere ci sono?**
   How many rooms are there?

10. **Quello al quinto piano è di quattro camere, cucina e bagno.**
    The one on the fifth floor has four rooms, a kitchen and a bath.

11. **Dà sulla strada?**
    Does it face the street?

12. **No, dà sul cortile.**
No, it faces the courtyard.

13. **E quello al secondo piano?**
And the one on the second floor?

14. **Quello al secondo piano ha una camera da letto, un salotto e una camera da pranzo.**
The one on the third floor has a bedroom, a living room, and a dining room.

15. **Dà anche sul cortile?**
Does it also face the courtyard?

16. **No, dà sulla strada.**
No, it faces the street.

17. **Quanto è l'affitto?**
How much is the rent?

18. **Il più grande costa quattromila euro al mese, più luce e gas.**
The larger one is 4,000 euros a month, plus light and gas.

19. **E quello ammobiliato?**
And the furnished one?

20. **Quello costa quattromilacinquecento euro al mese, tutto incluso.**
That one costs 4,500 euros a month, everything included.

21. **Com'è ammobiliato? In che condizioni sono i mobili?**
How is it furnished? In what condition is the furniture?

22. **I mobili sono moderni e sono in ottime condizioni.**
It's modern furniture and it's in excellent condition.

23. **La biancheria e i piatti sono inclusi?**
Are linen and silverware (dishes) included?

24. **Troverà tutto quello che Le occorre, perfino una batteria da cucina completa.**
You'll find everything you need, even a complete set of kitchen utensils.

25. **Bisogna firmare un contratto lungo?**
Do you have to sign a long lease?

26. **Per questo dovrà vedere l'amministratore.**
You'll have to see the rental agent for that.

27. **Quali sono le condizioni?**
What are the terms?

28. **Un mese anticipato e uno di deposito.**
One month's rent in advance and another month's rent as a deposit.

29. **È tutto?**
Is that all?

30. **Naturalmente, dovrà dare le Sue referenze.**
Of course you'll have to give references.

31. **A proposito, c'è l'ascensore?**
By the way, is there an elevator?

32. **No, non c'è ascensore.**
No, there is no elevator.

33. **Che peccato!**
That's too bad!

34. **A parte questo, la casa è molto moderna.**
Aside from that, the house is very modern.

35. **Che cosa vuol dire?**
What do you mean?

36. **C'è l'aria condizionata centrale.**
There's central air conditioning.

37. **C'è una lavanderia?**
Are there any laundry facilities?

38. **Naturalmente. E le camere da bagno sono state rimodernate di recente.**
Of course. And the bathrooms were recently remodeled.

39. **Si possono vedere gli appartamenti?**
Is it possible to see the apartments?

40. **Soltanto la mattina.**
Only in the morning.

41. **Va bene. Verrò domani mattina. Molte grazie.**
Very well. I'll come tomorrow morning. Thanks a lot.

42. **Di nulla. S'immagini. Felice di poterLa servire.**
Not at all. Don't mention it. Glad to be able to help you.

NOTES

1. *A* = in order to.

4. *Ce* is used instead of *ci*, because *ci, mi, ti, vi*, become *ce, me, te, ve* before *ne*.

5. *Me li:* as in 4.

9. *Ci sono* = there are.

11. Idiomatic expression. *Dare* = to give, but *dare su* = to face.

13. The first floor in Italy is called *pianterreno;* what we call the "second floor" in America is the *primo piano* in Italy.

21. *Il mobile* = piece of furniture. *I mobili* = the furniture *(pl.). La mobilia, il mobilio* = furniture *(sing.)*

22. *Ottime:* superlative of *buone (fem. pl.).*

23. *I piatti* includes dishes and silverware. *Il piatto da portata* = the serving dish. *L'argenteria* = the silverware.

26. *L'amministratore* = the manager.

30. Note article in front of *sue (possessive).*

31. The definite article is often used in Italian where the indefinite is used in English.

33. *Che peccato!* = What a sin!

35. *Vuol:* the final *e (vuole)* of verb forms is often dropped in speaking.

38. *sono state rimodernate* = have been remodeled.

42. *S'immagini* = imagine. A polite way to express "Don't mention it." Also: *Ma le pare.*

QUIZ 35

1. _____ (I've come) *a vedere l' appartamento.*
   a. *Sono venuta*
   b. *Sono*
   c. *Voglio*

2. *Quello* _____ (for) *affittare.*
   a. *in*
   b. *per*
   c. *da*

3. _____ (There are) *due.*
   a. *C'è*
   b. *Ce ne sono*
   c. *Sono*

4. *È* _____ (without) *mobili.*
   a. *con*
   b. *senza*
   c. *tra*

5. _____ (How much) *è l'affitto?*
   a. *Quando*
   b. *Quanto*
   c. *Troppo*

6. _____ (Does it face) *sulla strada?*
   a. *Guarda*
   b. *Faccia*
   c. *Dà*

7. *Dà* _____ (also) *sul giardino?*
   a. *altro*
   b. *anche*
   c. *poi*

8. _____ (It costs) *un milione ottocento mila lire.*
   a. *Costa*
   b. *Quanto*
   c. *Viene*

9. *Bisogna* _____ (sign) *un contratto?*
    a. *scrivere*
    b. *segnare*
    c. *firmare*
10. *La casa è* _____ (very) *moderna.*
    a. *molto*
    b. *tanto*
    c. *male*

ANSWERS

1—a; 2—c; 3—b; 4—b; 5—b; 6—c; 7—b; 8—a; 9—c;
10—a.

B. To Have: *AVERE*

io ho	I have
tu hai	you have
lui, lei, Lei ha	he, she has, you have
noi abbiamo	we have
voi avete	you have
loro hanno	they have

    a. *Avere* is also used in place of the English verb "to
    be" when talking about hunger, thirst, and other
    temporary conditions or feelings. *Avere* means "to
    have" in the sense of "to possess."

Ho questo.	I have this. I've got this.
Non ho nulla.	I don't have anything.
Lo ha Lei?	Do you have it?
Non l'ho.	I don't have it.
Ho tempo.	I have time.
Non ho denaro.	I don't have any money.
Non ho tempo.	I don't have any time.
Lui non ha amici.	He doesn't have any friends.
Ho fame.	I'm hungry.
Ho sete.	I'm thirsty.
Ho sonno.	I'm sleepy.

Ho freddo.	I'm cold.
Ho caldo.	I'm hot.
Ho ragione.	I'm right.
Lui non ha ragione.	He is not right.
Loro non hanno ragione.	They're wrong.
Ha *(Lei)* **degli amici a Roma?**	Do you have (any) friends in Rome?
Io non ho amici a Roma.	I don't have any friends in Rome.
Ha una sigaretta?	Do you have a cigarette? *(pol.)*
Io non ho sigarette.	I don't have any cigarettes.
Ha un fiammifero?	Do you have a light (a match)? *(pol.)*
Non ho fiammiferi.	I don't have any matches.
Ho vent'anni.	I'm twenty.
Ho mal di testa.	I have a headache.
Ho mal di denti.	I have a toothache.
Che cosa hai?	What's the matter with you?
Non ho nulla.	Nothing's the matter with me.
Quanto denaro ha?	How much money do you have?
Io non ho denaro (affatto).	I don't have any money (at all).
Ho molto da fare.	I have a lot to do.

b. Do I have it?

L'ho *(lo ho)* **io?**	Do I have it?
L'hai tu?	Do you have it? *(fam.)*
L'ha Lei?	Do you have it? *(polite)*
L'ha lui?	Does he have it?
L'abbiamo noi?	Do we have it?
L'avete voi?	Do you have it? *(plural)*
L'hanno loro?	Do they have it?

c. Don't I have it?

Non l'ho *(lo ho)* **io?**	Don't I have it?

Non l'hai tu?	Don't you have it? *(fam.)*
Non l'ha Lei?	Don't you have it? *(polite)*
Non l'ha lei?	Doesn't she have it?
Non l'abbiamo noi?	Don't we have it?
Non l' avete voi?	Don't you have it? *(pl.)*
Non l'hanno loro?	Don't they have it?

QUIZ 36

1. *Non ho denaro.*	a. I have a headache.
2. *Non ho nulla.*	b. Don't you have it?
3. *Lui non ha ragione.*	c. I don't have it.
4. *Ho sonno.*	d. I'm cold.
5. *L'ha lui?*	e. I'm hot.
6. *Non l'ho.*	f. I don't have any money.
7. *Ho fame.*	g. Does he have it?
8. *Ho freddo.*	h. He's not right.
9. *Ho vent' anni.*	i. I'm thirsty.
10. *Non l'ha Lei?*	j. I have a lot to do.
11. *Io devo andare.*	k. I don't have anything.
12. *Ho caldo.*	l. I'm sleepy.
13. *Ho sete.*	m. I'm hungry.
14. *Ho mal di testa.*	n. I have to go.
15. *Ho molto da fare.*	o. I'm twenty years old.

ANSWERS

1—f; 2—k; 3—h; 4—l; 5—g; 6—c; 7—m; 8—d; 9—o;
10—b; 11—n; 12—e; 13—i; 14—a; 15—j.

LESSON 37

A. COULD YOU GIVE ME SOME INFORMATION?

1. **Mi scusi.**
   Pardon me. *(polite)*

2. **In che cosa posso servirLa?**
   What can I do for you?

3. **Mi potrebbe dare alcune informazioni?**
   Could you give me some information?

4. **Con molto piacere.**
   Gladly. (With much pleasure.)

5. **Io non conosco questa città e non mi posso orientare.**
   I don't know this city, and I can't find my way around.

6. **Bene, è abbastanza semplice.**
   Well, it's quite simple.

7. **Come vede, io sono straniera.**
   As you see, I'm a foreigner (here).

8. **In questo caso Le mostrerò la città.**
   In that case I'll show you the town.

9. **La ringrazierò moltissimo. Lo apprezzerò molto.**
   I'd be very grateful to you. I'd appreciate that a lot.

10. **Vede quel gran palazzo all'angolo?**
    Do you see that large building on the corner?

11. **Quello con la bandiera?**
    The one with the flag?

12. **Esattamente. Quello è la Posta Centrale.**
    Exactly. That's the Main Post Office.

    Di fronte dall'altro lato della strada . . .
    Opposite, on the other side of the street . . .

13. **Dove?**
Where?

14. **Da quella parte. Vede quell'altro palazzo con gli archi?**
Over there. Do you see that other building with arches?

15. **Oh, sì, adesso lo vedo.**
Oh, yes, now I see it.

16. **Quella è la Galleria Colonna.**
That's the Colonna Gallery.

17. **La vedo. . . . A proposito, qual'è il nome di questa piazza?**
I see it. . . . By the way, what's the name of this square?

18. **Piazza San Silvestro.**
Saint Sylvester Square.

19. **Dov'è la Questura?**
Where is the Police Station?

20. **In fondo a quella strada, a destra.**
At the end of the street, to the right.

21. **E se non la trovo?**
What if I miss it (if I don't find it)?

22. **Non si preoccupi.**
Don't worry. *(polite)*

È un gran palazzo grigio, con due guardie di fronte all'entrata.
It's a big, gray building with two guards in front of the entrance.

Vede quel negozio?
You see that store?

23. **Quale negozio? Quello a sinistra?**
Which store? The one on the left?

24. **Esattamente. Quello che ha quel grosso globo di vetro verde in vetrina.**
Right. The one with the large green glass globe in the window.

25. **È una barbieria?**
It's a barbershop?

26. **No, è una farmacia.**
No, it's a pharmacy.

Al lato del negozio c'è la casa del dottore.
The doctor lives right next door. (Next to the store is the doctor's house.)

Il suo nome è sulla porta.
His name is on the door.

27. **Ha l'ufficio nella stessa casa in cui abita?**
Does he have his office there as well? (Does he have his office in the same house in which he lives?)

28. **Sì, ma tutte le mattine va all'ospedale.**
Yes, but he spends every morning at the hospital.

29. **Dov'è l'ospedale?**
Where is the hospital?

30. **Per raggiungere l'ospedale, Lei deve camminare per Corso Umberto, verso Piazza del Popolo.**
To reach the hospital, you must take the Umberto Corso (Avenue) toward Popolo Square.

Alla penultima strada a sinistra si trova Via San Giacomo, e l'Ospedale San Giacomo è là.

A block before reaching the Square, you will come to Saint Giacomo (James) Street on the left, and the Saint Giacomo hospital is there.

31. **Come posso ritornare al mio albergo?**
How can I get back to my hotel?

32. **Vada per questa strada. Lo vede là, dopo il . . .**
Go this way. You see it there, next to the . . .

33. **. . . cinema? Non è così?**
. . . movies? Right? (Isn't it so?)

34. **Esatto.**
Yes. (Exactly.)

35. **Ora ho capito.**
Now I understand.

36. **Perchè non si compra una guida?**
Why don't you buy yourself a guidebook?

37. **Non è una cattiva idea. Dove posso comprarla?**
That's not a bad idea. Where can I buy one?

38. **Alla stazione, oppure in qualsiasi edicola.**
At the train station, or at any newsstand.

39. **È lontana da qui la stazione?**
Is the station far from here?

40. **La stazione si trova in Piazza Cinquecento.**
The station is in Cinquecento (Five Hundred) Square.

41. **Dove si trova un edicola qui vicino?**
Where's there a newsstand near here?

42. **Ce n'è una all'angolo.**
There's one on the corner.

43. **La ringrazio molto.**
Thank you very much. (I thank you very much.)

44. **Non c'è di che.**
Not at all.

    Sono molto lieto di esserLe stato utile.
I'm very glad to have been of help to you. (I'm very glad to have been useful to you.)

45. **Sono stata molto fortunata di averLa incontrata.**
I was certainly lucky to meet you.

    Lei conosce questa città molto bene.
You really know this town very well.

46. **Non si sorprenda. Io sono il Sindaco.**
It's not surprising. I'm the mayor.

NOTES

2. *In che cosa posso servirLa?* = In what thing can I serve you?

3. *Potrebbe:* conditional of *potere*.

5. *Orientarsi* = to orient oneself.

6. *Abbastanza* = enough.

9. *Apprezzerò:* future of *apprezzare*.

10. *Gran:* abbreviated form of *grande*.

12. *La posta centrale* = main post office. *La posta* = the mail.

14. *Palazzo* = building; also *edificio*. *Il palazzo* can also be "a palace."

24. In Italy, pharmacies usually have a green globe, or a big vase, in the window.

25. *La barbiera* = the barber shop; *un barbiere* = a barber; can also be called *parrucchiere*.

30. *La penultima strada* = the street before the last. In Italy, people count by streets, not by blocks. There is actually no real word for block, although *isolato* is sometimes used. *Caseggiato* is a group of buildings that might sometimes correspond to an American block.

33. *Cinema* is really the "Movie Theater." The movie (film) is called *la pellicola*, or *il film*.

35. *Ho capito* = I have understood. This is the past tense, but this expression is often used instead of *capisco* with the same meaning.

37. *Cattiva* = bad, meaning literally "ugly." *Brutto* is also often used with the meaning of "bad." *Che brutta idea!* = What a bad idea!

44. *Non c'è di che.* (There is nothing about it . . . You are welcome.) A polite formula to use in answer to *grazie* (thank you). Another currently used expression is *prego. Sono molto lieto(a) di esserle stato(a) utile.* (I am very glad to have been of help to you.) A polite expression.

46. *Non si sorprenda.* = Don't surprise yourself.

QUIZ 37

1. *È molto _____ (simple).*
   a. *poco*
   b. *semplice*
   c. *città*

2. *Le farò vedere la _____ (city).*
   a. *caso*
   b. *città*
   c. *orientare*

3. *Questo grande palazzo all' _____ (corner).*
   a. *angolo*
   b. *via*
   c. *ufficio postale*

4. *Questo è l' _____ (post office).*
   a. *via*
   b. *ufficio postale*
   c. *altro*

5. *Vede questo _____ (store)?*
   a. *destra*
   b. *negozio*
   c. *barbiere*

6. *Nella casa vicina c'è un _____ (doctor).*
   a. *dottore*
   b. *farmacia*
   c. *nome*

7. *Il suo nome è sulla _____ (door).*
   a. *stesso*
   b. *porta*
   c. *clinica*

8. *Ha l'ufficio nella stessa _____ (house) in cui vive?*
   a. *dopo*
   b. *lato*
   c. *casa*

9. *Un poco* _____ (before) *di arrivare alla strada principale.*
   a. *dopo*
   b. *prima*
   c. *passata*

10. *Dove posso* _____ (buy) *questo?*
    a. *comprare*
    b. *guida*
    c. *stazione*

ANSWERS

1—b; 2—b; 3—a; 4—b; 5—b; 6—a; 7—b; 8—c; 9—b; 10—a.

LESSON 38

A. GREETING AN OLD FRIEND

1. **P: Oh, eccoti qui! Come stai?**
   Oh, there you are! How are you?

2. **L: E tu come stai?**
   How are you?

3. **P: Non sei troppo stanco del tuo viaggio?**
   Not too tired from your trip?

4. **L: Niente affatto!**
   Not at all!

5. **P: Desidero presentarti a mia moglie.**
   I'd like you to meet my wife.

6. **L: Con molto piacere.**
   I'd be very happy to.

7. **P: Cara, ti presento Giovanni Lanzi.**
   This is Giovanni Lanzi, dear.

8. **L: Molto felice di conoscerLa.**
   I'm very happy to know you.

9. Sig: **Molto piacere.**
   Glad to know you.

10. **L: E'stato un vero piacere per me di rivederti.**
    It's been a real pleasure to see you again.

11. **P: Anche per me. Tu non sei cambiato affatto.**
    I feel the same way about it. (For me, too.) You haven't
    changed a bit.

12. **L: E neanche tu.**
    Neither have you.

13. Sig: **Cosa pensa la signora Lanzi degli Stati Uniti?**
    How does Mrs. Lanzi like the United States?

14. **L: Le piacciono moltissimo.**
    She likes it a lot.

15. Sig: **Deve essere molto diverso da Roma, no?**
    It must be very different from Rome, isn't it?

16. **L: Negli Stati Uniti, decisamente, ci sono molte cose
    strane!**
    There certainly are lots of very curious things in the
    United States.

17. Sig: **Per esempio?**
    For example?

18. L: **Per esempio, non mi sarebbe mai venuto in mente di far colazione in una farmacia!**
For example, it certainly would never have come to my mind to have lunch in a pharmacy!

19. P: **Ma vuoi scherzare!**
You are joking!

20. L: **Niente affatto. Sto dicendo sul serio.**
Not at all. I'm very serious.

21. Sig: **Suvvia, ci racconti. Lei vuol dire che si può fare colazione … in una farmacia?**
Come, tell us about it. You mean one can have lunch… in a pharmacy?

22. L: **Certamente, signora. Lei può anche ordinare un bistecca.**
Naturally, madam. You can even have a steak.

23. P: **In una farmacia?**
In a pharmacy?

24. L: **Sì, in una farmacia, e con un ottimo gelato per dolce.**
Yes, in a pharmacy, and with excellent ice cream for dessert.

25. Sig: **Ma l'odore della farmacia, non disturba?**
But the smell of the pharmacy, doesn't that bother you?

26. L: **Non, c'è nessun odore nelle nostre …**
There isn't any smell in our …

27. P: **Farmacie?**
Pharmacies?

28. **L: In America, non le chiamano farmacie, ma drug-stores.**
In America, they don't call them pharmacies, but drug-stores.

29. **P: Oh … qui sta l'inganno! Le chiamano con nomi differenti!**
Oh … that's the trick! They give them a different name!

30. **Sig: Ma come può questo cambiare le cose?**
But how does that change things?

31. **P: Allora, non è più una farmacia!**
Then it's no longer a pharmacy!

32. **L: Nel "drugstore" si vendono anche molte altre cose, come giocattoli, francobolli, sigarette, caramelle …**
You also find other things in a drugstore; toys, stamps, cigarettes, candy …

33. **P: Questo è veramente buffo!**
That's really very funny!

34. **L: … libri, carta da scrivere, utensili da cucina, articoli da toletta, e altro.**
… books, stationery, cooking utensils, toilet articles, and what-have-you.

35. **P: Allora, è un bazar?**
It's a bazaar, then?

36. **L: No, mio caro, è sempre un "drugstore!"**
No, my dear, it's (still) a drugstore!

NOTES

2. The *tu (fam.)* pronoun is used because two friends are speaking.

4. *Niente affatto* = nothing done (*niente a-fatto:* from *fare*).

18. *Sarebbe venuto* = It would have come. (*Venuto:* past part. of *venire*. Double negation because the sentence begins with *non*.)

19. *Scherzare* = to joke. *Lo scherzo* = the joke. Other words are *la barzelletta, la freddura*.

20. *Sul serio* = on the serious side, or seriously.

21. *Suvvia* = Come on! The word is really composed of two expressions meaning "come on": *su* and *via*. Here the two words are linked by an extra *v*.

24. *Ottimo* is really the superlative of *buono*, meaning "excellent".

26. An example of the double negation often used in Italian.

29. *L'inganno* is also "deceit" from the verb *ingannare* (to deceive).

QUIZ 38

1. _____ (How) *stai?*
   a. *Qui*
   b. *Dove*
   c. *Come*

2. *Non sei troppo* _____ (tired) *dal tuo viaggio?*
   a. *affatto*
   b. *felice*
   c. *stanco*

3. *Desidero presentarti a mia* _____ (wife).
   a. *moglie*
   b. *molto*
   c. *piacere*

4. *È stato un vero* _____ (pleasure) *per me.*
   a. *cambiato*
   b. *piacere*
   c. *conoscere*

5. *Le piacciono* _____ (a lot).
   a. *moltissimo*
   b. *poco*
   c. *diverso*

6. *Ci sono molte* _____ (things) *strane!*
   a. *vero*
   b. *decisamente*
   c. *cose*

7. *Sto dicendo sul* _____ (serious).
   a. *serio*
   b. *scherzare*
   c. *venuto*

8. *Non le* _____ (call) *farmacie.*
   a. *chiamano*
   b. *inganno*
   c. *cambiare*

9. _____ (Then) *è un bazar?*
   a. *Allora*
   b. *Anche*
   c. *Sempre*

10. *Nel "drugstore" si vendono* _____ (stamps).
    a. *giocattoli*
    b. *francobolli*
    c. *caramelle*

LESSON 39

A. SOME IMPORTANT IRREGULAR VERBS

1. *Potere* = to be able

PRESENT	PRESENT PERFECT	FUTURE	PAST PARTICIPLE
io posso	io ho potuto	io potrò	potuto
tu puoi	tu hai potuto	tu potrai	
lui può	lui ha potuto	lui potrà	
lei può	lei ha potuto	lei potrà	
noi possiamo	noi abbiamo potuto	noi potremo	
voi potete	voi avete potuto	voi potrete	
Loro possono	Loro hanno potuto	Loro potranno	
loro possono	loro hanno potuto	loro potranno	

Posso?	May I? Can I?
Dove posso mandare un facsìmile?	Where can I send a fax?
Potrai venire questa sera?	Will you be able to come tonight?
Posso parlare con lui?	May I speak with him?

2. *Dovere* = to have to

PRESENT	PRESENT PERFECT	FUTURE	PAST PARTICIPLE
io devo	io ho dovuto	io dovrò	dovuto
tu devi	tu hai dovuto	tu dovrai	
lui deve	lui ha dovuto	lui dovrà	
noi dobbiamo	noi abbiamo dovuto	noi dovremo	
voi dovete	voi avete dovuto	voi dovrete	
loro devono	loro hanno dovuto	loro dovranno	

Devo farlo.	I must do it.
Io devo andare.	I have to leave.
Io ti devo cinque dollari.	I owe you five dollars.
Dovrei *(conditional)* andarci.	I should go there.

3. *Volere* = to want

PRESENT	PRESENT PERFECT	FUTURE	PAST PARTICIPLE
io voglio	io ho voluto	io vorrò	voluto
tu vuoi	tu hai voluto	tu vorrai	
lui vuole	lui ha voluto	lui vorrà	
noi vogliamo	noi abbiamo voluto	noi vorremo	
voi volete	voi avete voluto	voi vorrete	
loro vogliono	loro hanno voluto	loro vorranno	

Voler bene a qualcuno.	To like someone.
Voglio farlo.	I want to do it.
Vorrei *(conditional)* finire.	I would like to finish.

4. *Sapere* = to know

PRESENT	PRESENT PERFECT	FUTURE	PAST PARTICIPLE
io so	io ho saputo	io saprò	saputo
tu sai	tu hai saputo	tu saprai	
lui sa	lui ha saputo	lui saprà	
noi sappiamo	noi abbiamo saputo	noi sapremo	
voi sapete	voi avete saputo	voi saprete	
loro sanno	loro hanno saputo	loro sapranno	

Lo so che è vero.	I know it's true.
Hai saputo la notizia?	Did you hear the news?
Loro lo sapranno in tempo.	They'll find out in time.

5. *Andare* = to go

PRESENT	PRESENT PERFECT	FUTURE	PAST PARTICIPLE
io vado	io sono andato(-a)	io andrò	andato
tu vai	tu sei andato(-a)	tu andrai	
lui va	lui è andato	lui andrà	
noi andiamo	noi siamo andati(-e)	noi andremo	
voi andate	voi siete andati(-e)	voi andrete	
loro vanno	loro sono andati(-e)	loro andranno	

Sono andato a piedi.	I walked. (I went on foot.)
Andremo insieme.	We'll go together.

Vada presto! *(pol. imperative)*   Go quickly!
Andiamo!   Let's go!

6. *Venire* = to come

| | PRESENT | | PAST |
PRESENT	PERFECT	FUTURE	PARTICIPLE
io vengo	io sono venut*o*(-a)	io verrò	**venuto**
tu vieni	tu sei venuto(-a)	tu verrai	
lui viene	lui è venuto	lui verrà	
noi veniamo	noi siamo venuti(-*e*)	noi verremo	
voi venite	voi siete venuti(-*e*)	voi verrete	
loro vengono	loro sono venuti(-*e*)	loro verranno	

Vieni con me, non è   You're coming with me, aren't
  vero?   you?
Viene sempre da me.   He always comes to my house.
Quando verrà lei?   When will she come?
Vengono spesso in città. They often come to the city.
Venga *(imperative)*   Come tomorrow at about
  domani verso le tre.   three.

LESSON 40

A. FUN IN ITALIAN

UN'OTTIMISTA

Il capo di un'importante casa commerciale, leggendo una
richiesta di lavoro, si meraviglia moltissimo nel notare che
il richiedente, pur non avendo esperienza, domanda uno
stipendio eccessivo.

-Non Le sembra di richiedere uno stipendio troppo alto, considerando la Sua poca esperienza in merito?

-Tutt'altro, assumere un lavoro del quale non si sa assolutamente nulla, è cosa molto più difficile, e dovrebbe essere pagata molto meglio.

AN OPTIMIST

The head of an important firm, looking at a job application, is astonished when he notices that the applicant, though lacking experience, is asking for a high salary.

"Doesn't it seem to you that you are asking for an excessive salary, considering the little experience you have?"

"On the contrary, work performed by one who knows nothing about it is more difficult and should be better paid."

NOTES

1. *Si meraviglia moltissimo* = is very much amazed.
   Meravigliarsi: to wonder, to be astonished, to be surprised.

2. *Nel* is a contraction for *in il*.

3. *Pur* = although. (Always followed by the participle.)

4. *Non le sembra di richiedere?* = Does it not seem to you to ask? *Le sembra* = It seems to you. *Mi sembra* = It seems to me. *Ci sembra* = It seems to us.

5. *tutt' altro* = everything else, on the contrary.

6. *dovrebbe:* condit. of *dovere* (*dovrebbe* = it should be).

UNA PERDITA DI POCA IMPORTANZA

CLIENTE: Signora, per favore, mi dia una copia del "Messaggero." Non ho spiccioli. Può cambiarmi queste cinque euro?

GIORNALAIA: Può pagarmi domani.

CLIENTE: E se morissi questa notte?
GIORNALAIA:Oh, non sarebbe davvero una grande
perdita.

A MINOR LOSS

CUSTOMER: Miss, could you please give me a copy of the
Messenger? I don't have any change. Could you change
this bill of five euros for me?
NEWSSTAND ATTENDANT: You can pay for it tomorrow.
CUSTOMER: What if I die tonight?
ATTENDANT: Oh, it wouldn't be a very great loss.

NOTES

1. *Spiccioli* = change, "little money."

2. *E se morissi:* if I were to die (past subjunctive of *morire*).

3. *Sarebbe:* conditional of "to be" (It would [not] be).

UNA LEZIONE DI ETICHETTA

Pietro e Giovanni vanno a mangiare in un ristorante.
Entrambi ordinano una bistecca. Il cameriere li serve
poco dopo. Pietro afferra subito la bistecca più grande.
Giovanni, seccato, gli dice:
   -Come sei maleducato! Ti servi per primo e ti prendi
anche il pezzo più grande.
   Pietro gli risponde:
   -Se tu fossi stato al mio posto, quale pezzo avresti scelto?
   -Il più piccolo, naturalmente.
   -E allora, perchè ti lamenti? Non lo hai il più piccolo?

A LESSON IN ETIQUETTE

Peter and John go to a restaurant to eat. They both order
steak. The waiter brings the steaks to them shortly afterward. Peter grabs the larger steak. John says to him
angrily:

"What bad manners you have! You helped yourself first and you took the larger piece."

Pietro answers:

"If you had been in my place, which piece would you have taken?

"The smaller, of course."

"Then what are you complaining about? You have it, don't you?"

NOTES

1. *Entrambi* = both of them; also *tutti e due*.

2. *Sei:* familiar form of the present "to be." (Pietro and Giovanni are friends.)

3. *Se tu fossi stato* = if you had been. (The pluperfect subjunctive is used in this case to indicate a condition contrary to fact.)

4. *Avresti scelto:* past conditional of *scegliere;* expresses the second part of the conditional sentence. *Se io fossi stato in quel ristorante, avrei ordinato pollo arrosto.* If I had been in that restaurant, I would have ordered roast chicken.

5. *Ti lamenti* = you lament yourself. *Lamentarsi:* reflexive verb meaning "to lament," "to complain."

B. IMPORTANT SIGNS

Signori or *Uomini*	Men
Signore or *Donne*	Women
Gabinetto	Toilet
Chiuso	Closed
Aperto	Open
Proibito fumare	No Smoking
Vietato fumare	No Smoking
Vietato l'ingresso	No Admittance

Bussare	Knock
Suonare il campanello	Ring
Strada privata	Private Street
Per informazioni rivolgersi qui	Inquire Within
Alt! Stop! Fermo!	Stop!
Via libera!	Go!
Attenzione!	Look Out!
Pericolo	Danger
Rallentare	Go Slow
Svolta obbligata	Detour
Attenzione	Caution (Look Out)
Mantenere la destra	Keep to the Right
Ponte	Bridge
Divieto di sosta	No Parking
Ufficio controllo	Check Room
Cambio	Money Exchange
Informazioni	Information
Sala d' aspetto	Waiting Room
Vietato sporgesi (dalla finestra)	Don't Lean Out (of the window)
Treno merci	Freight Car
Binario ferroviario	Railroad Track
Direttissimo	Express
Accelerato (locale)	Local
Fermata	Stop (bus, streetcar, etc.)
Vietata l' affissione	Post No Bills
In riparazione	Under Repair
Entrata	Entrance
Uscita	Exit
Camere ammobiliate	Furnished Rooms
Appartamenti	Apartments
Pittura fresca	Wet Paint
Incrocio	Crossroads/Intersection
Macelleria	Butcher (Butcher's Shop)
Panificio	Bakery

Latteria	Dairy
Sartoria	Tailor Shop (also for women)
Calzoleria	Shoe Store
Barbiere	Barbershop (barber)
Salumeria	Grocer
Farmacia	Pharmacy, Drugstore
Pasticceria	Candy Store
Cartoleria	Stationery Store
Cassetta delle lettere	Mail Box
Buca delle lettere	Mail Box
Bar	Bar
Questura	Police Station
Vini	Wines
Distributore benzina	Gas Station
Libreria	Bookstore
Commune municipo	City Hall
Bibite—Gelati	Drinks—Ice Cream
Acqua fredda	Cold Water
Acqua calda	Hot Water

QUIZ 39

1. *Entrata*
2. *Svolta obbligata*
3. *Vietato sporgersi (dalla finestra)*
4. *Chiuso*
5. *Aperto*
6. *Vietato fumare*
7. *Espresso*
8. *Divieto di sosta*
9. *Uscita*
10. *Informazioni*

a. No Smoking
b. Express
c. No Parking
d. Open
e. Exit
f. Information
g. Detour
h. Entrance
i. Closed
j. Don't Lean Out (of the window)

ANSWERS

1—h; 2—g; 3—j; 4—i; 5—d; 6—a; 7—b; 8—c; 9—e; 10—f.

FINAL QUIZ

1. _____ (Tell me) *dov'è la stazione.*
   a. *Mi permetta*
   b. *Mi dica*
   c. *Mi porti*

2. _____ (Can) *dirmi dov'è l'ufficio postale?*
   a. *Può*
   b. *Avere*
   c. *Costo*

3. *Dove* _____ (is) *un buon ristorante?*
   a. *fare*
   b. *c'è*
   c. *oggi*

4. _____ (Bring me) *un po' di pane.*
   a. *ConoscerLa*
   b. *Mi permetta*
   c. *Mi porti*

5. _____ (I need) *di sapone.*
   a. *Ho bisogno*
   b. *Avere*
   c. *Permette*

6. _____ (I would like) *un po' più di carne.*
   a. *Mi porti*
   b. *Mi manca*
   c. *Desidero*

7. *La* _____ (I introduce) *alla mia amica.*
   a. *presento*
   b. *ho*
   c. *venga*

8. *Dov'* _____ (is) *il libro?*
   a. *è*
   b. *quello*
   c. *questo*

9. _____ (Please) *parli lentamente.*
   a. *La bontà*
   b. *Per piacere*
   c. *Il favore*

10. _____ (Do you understand) *l'italiano?*
    a. *Comprendo*
    b. *Parla*
    c. *Comprende*

11. _____ (Go) *là.*
    a. *Vada*
    b. *Parla*
    c. *Essere*

12. _____ (Come) *subito.*
    a. *Venga*
    b. *Vado*
    c. *Andiamo*

13. *Come si* _____ (call) *Lei?*
    a. *lavare*
    b. *chiama*
    c. *chiamano*

14. *Che giorno della* _____ (week) *è oggi?*
    a. *settimana*
    b. *mese*
    c. *anno*

15. *Che* _____ (time) *è?*
    a. *ora*
    b. *adesso*
    c. *ho*

16. *Non* _____ (I have) *sigarette.*
    a. *tempo*
    b. *ho*
    c. *avere*

17. _____ (Do you want) *della frutta?*
    a. *Potrebbe*
    b. *Ha lei*
    c. *Desidera*

18. _____ (Allow me) *di presentaLa al mio amico.*
    a. *Dare*
    b. *Mi permetta*
    c. *Mi porti*

19. _____ (I want) *scrivere una lettera*.
    a. *Desidera*
    b. *Desidero*
    c. *Mi permetta*

20. *Quanto* _____ (costs) *un a telefonata per Milano?*
    a. *costa*
    b. *costare*
    c. *conto*

21. *Desideriamo fare* _____ (breakfast).
    a. *colazione*
    b. *cena*
    c. *pranzo*

22. *È l'* _____ (1:45).
    a. *una a trenta*
    b. *una e quarantacinque*
    c. *una e quindici*

23. *Venga* _____ (tomorrow morning).
    a. *ieri mattina*
    b. *domani mattina*
    c. *domani a mezzogiorno*

24. *In che* _____ (can I) *servirLa?*
    a. *può*
    b. *posso*
    c. *possono*

25. *Non* _____ (has) *importanza*.
    a. *avere*
    b. *ha*
    c. *avuto*

ANSWERS

1—b; 2—a; 3—b; 4—c; 5—a; 6—c; 7—a; 8—a; 9—a;
10—c; 11—a; 12—a; 13—b; 14—a; 15—a; 16—b; 17—c;
18—b; 19—b; 20—a; 21—a; 22—b; 23—b; 24—b; 25—b.

SUMMARY OF ITALIAN GRAMMAR

1. ALPHABET

LETTER	NAME	LETTER	NAME	LETTER	NAME
a	*a*	h	*acca*	q	*qu*
b	*bi*	i	*i*	r	*erre*
c	*ci*	l	*elle*	s	*esse*
d	*di*	m	*emme*	t	*ti*
e	*e*	n	*enne*	u	*u*
f	*effe*	o	*o*	v	*vu*
g	*gi*	p	*pi*	z	*zeta*

2. PRONUNCIATION

SIMPLE VOWELS

a	as in *ah* or *father*
e	as in *day, ace*
i	as in *machine, police*
o	as in *no, note*
u	as in *rule*

VOWEL COMBINATIONS

ai	ai in *aisle*
au	ou in *out*
ei	ay-ee
eu	ay-oo
ia	ya in *yard*
ie	ye in *yes*
io	yo in *yoke*
iu	you
oi	oy in *boy*
ua	wah

ue	way
ui	oo-ee
uo	oo-oh

h	is never pronounced
ll	⎧ When two consonants occur in
mm	the middle of a word, they are
	both pronounced.
nn	Notice the difference between
	the following:
rr	*caro,* dear, *carro,* truck
ss	*casa,* house, *cassa,* case
	⎩ *pala,* shovel, *palla,* ball

1. *ci, ce* is pronounced like the English *ch* in *chair:*

cacciatore   hunter

2. *ch* before *e* and *i* is pronounced like the English *k* in *key:*

chitarra   guitar

3. *gi, ge* is pronounced like *j* in *jail:*

generoso   generous

4. *gh* before *e* and *i* is pronounced like the English *g* in *gate:*

ghirlanda   garland

5. *gli.* The closest English approximation is the combination *lli* as in *million:*

figlio   son   *paglia*   straw

6. *gn* is always pronounced as one letter, somewhat like the English *ni* in *onion* or *ny* in *canyon:*

segno	sign	*Spagna*	Spain

7. *sc* before *e* and *i* is pronounced like the English *sh* in *shoe:*

scendere	(to) descend	*sciroppo*	syrup

8. *sc* before *a, o,* and *u* is pronounced like the English *sk* in *sky:*

scuola	school	*scarpa*	shoe

3. STRESS

1. Words of two syllables are generally stressed on the first syllable, unless the other one bears an accent mark:

lapis	pencil	*città*	city
penna	pen	*virtù*	virtue
meta	goal	*metà*	half

2. Words of more than two syllables are generally stressed either on the syllable before the last, or on the syllable before that:

ancora	more	*ancora*	anchor
dolore	grief	*amore*	love
scatola	box	*automobile*	car

4. USE OF THE DEFINITE ARTICLE

il, l' and *lo* (masc. sing.)   *la* and *l'* (fem. sing.)
i and *gli* (masc. pl.)   *le* (fem. pl.)

There are instances in which Italian uses a definite article where no article is used in English:

Il tempo è denaro.	Time is money.
La vita è piena di guai.	Life is full of troubles.
I lupi sono feroci.	Wolves are ferocious.
I cani sono fedeli.	Dogs are faithful.
L'oro è un metallo prezioso.	Gold is a precious metal.
Il ferro è duro.	Iron is hard.
Gli affari sono affari.	Business is business.
La necessità non conosce legge.	Necessity knows no law.

Remember that in Italian you generally find the definite article in front of a possessive adjective or pronoun:

Il mio libro è nero, il tuo rosso. My book is black, yours red.

But with nouns indicating a family member in the singular, no article is used with the possessive adjective:

mio padre	my father
tuo fratello	your brother
nostro zio	our uncle

With *loro* (their or your), with *nonno, nonna* (grandfather and grandmother), and with *papà, mamma* (daddy, mama), or when the relationship noun is modified, the definite article is used with the possessive:

la loro mamma	their mother
il vostro nonno	your grandfather
il mio padre generoso	my generous father

In expressions like the following, Italian uses the definite article:

Tre volte la settimana	Three times a week.
Due dollari la libbra.	Two dollars a pound.

The definite article is used when talking about parts of the human body.

Il signore ha il naso lungo.	The gentleman has a long nose.

The definite article is always used with expressions of time:

Sono le due.	It is two o'clock.

With some geographical expressions:

L'Europa è un continente.	Europe is a continent.
Il Tevere è un fiume.	The Tiber is a river.

5. USE OF THE INDEFINITE ARTICLE

Un, uno, una, un'

Italian uses no indefinite article in cases like the following ones:

Io sono maestro.	I am a teacher.
Che donna!	What a woman!
mezzo chilo	half a kilo
cento uomini	a hundred men

6. THE PLURAL

There is no special plural form for:

1. Nouns with a written accent on the last vowel:

la città	the city
le città	the cities
la virtù	the virtue
le virtù	the virtues

2. Nouns ending in *i* in the singular, and almost all the nouns in *ie*:

il brindisi	the toast
i brindisi	the toasts
la crisi	the crisis
le crisi	the crises
la superficie	the surface
le superficie	the surfaces

3. Nouns ending in a consonant:

il bar	the bar
i bar	the bars
il gas	the gas
i gas	the gases

7. THE PARTITIVE

1. The partitive can be expressed in Italian in several ways:

    a. With the preposition *di* + a form of the definite article *il, lo, la:*

Io mangio del pane.	I eat some (of the) bread.
Io mangio della carne.	I eat some meat.
Io prendo dello zucchero.	I take some sugar.
Io leggo dei libri.	I read some books.
Io scrivo degli esercizi.	I write some exercises.
Io compro delle sedie.	I buy some chairs.

b. By using *qualche* (only with singular nouns):

Io scrivo qualche lettera.	I write a few letters.
Io leggo qualche giornale.	I read a few (some) newspapers.

c. By using *alcuni, alcune* (only in the plural):

Io ho alcuni amici.	I have a few friends.
Io scrivo alcune poesie.	I write a few poems.

d. By using *un po' di:*

Io prendo un po' di zucchero.	I'll take some sugar.

2. In some cases, especially if the sentence is negative, Italian does not use any partitive at all:

Io non mangio cipolle.	I don't eat onions.

8. ADJECTIVES

1. Most singular adjectives end in *-o* for the masculine and *-a* for the feminine:

un caro amico	a dear friend *(masc.)*
una cara amica	a dear friend *(fem.)*

2. Most plural adjectives end in *-i* for the masculine and *-e* for the feminine:

cari amici	dear friends *(masc.)*
care amiche	dear friends *(fem.)*

3. Some singular adjectives end in *-e* in the masculine and in the feminine:

| *un uomo gentile* | a kind man |
| *una donna gentile* | a kind woman |

In the plural these same adjectives end in *i* in both the masculine and the feminine:

| *uomini gentili* | kind men |
| *donne gentili* | kind women |

9. POSITION OF THE ADJECTIVE

In general, adjectives follow the noun. Some common exceptions are: *buono* (good), *cattivo* (bad), *nuovo* (new), *bello* (beautiful), and *brutto* (ugly).

la musica italiana	Italian music
il libro nero	the black book
una brutta giomata	an awful day
un nuovo libro	a new book

Possessive adjectives, demonstrative adjectives, numerals, and indefinite adjectives generally precede the noun:

il mio amico	my friend
questo libro	this book
due penne	two pens
alcuni signori	a few men

10. COMPARISON

(così) . . . come	as . . . as
tanto . . . quanto	as much/as many . . . as
più . . . di or che	more . . . than
meno . . . di or che	fewer/less . . . than

| *Il mio appartamento è (così) grande come il tuo.* | My apartment is as large as yours. |

Ho tanto denaro quanto ne ho bisogno.	I have as much money as I need.
Hanno tanti amici quanto vogliano.	They have as many friends as they want.

After *più* and *meno*, either *di* or *che* can be used, but if the comparison is between two adjectives, or if there is a preposition, only *che* can be used:

Franco è più studioso di (or che) Carlo.	Frank is more studious than Charles.
Giacomo è più studioso che intelligente.	James is more studious than intelligent.
Ci sono meno fanciulli in campagna che in città.	There are fewer children in the country than in the city.

If the second term of the comparison is expressed by a clause, *di quello che* must be used.

Studia puì di quello che tu pensi.	He studies more than you think.

If the second term of the comparison is expressed by a pronoun, the object form is used:

Lui è più alto di me.	He is taller than I.
Io sono meno ricco di te.	I am less rich than you.
Lei è così coraggiosa che lui.	She is as brave as he.

SPECIAL USES OF THE COMPARATIVE

Some expressions with the comparative:

ancora del (dello, della, dei, etc.)	more

un po' più di	a little more
altro, -a, -i, -e	more
Voglio ancora del pane.	I want more bread.
Prendo un po' più di carne.	I take a little more meat.
Compriamo altri libri.	We buy more books.
non più	no more (quantity)
non più	no longer (time)
Volete di più? No, non vogliamo di piu.	Do you want more? No, we don't want any more.
Lei non canta più.	She doesn't sing any more.
Tanto meglio!	Great! (So much the better.)
Tanto peggio!	Too bad! (So much the worse.)

11. RELATIVE SUPERLATIVE

The relative superlative (the most/the least/the . . . -est) is formed by placing the appropriate definite article before *più* or *meno*. Of/in is translated with *di*, whether by itself or combined with the definite article:

Quest' uomo è il più ricco del mondo.	This man is the richest in the world.
Lei è la piu famosa delle sorelle.	She is the most famous of the sisters.
Marco è il meno timido di tutti.	Marco is the least timid of all.

The subjunctive often follows the superlative:

È il quadro più bello che io abbia mai visto.	It's the most beautiful painting I have ever seen.

With the superlative of adverbs, the definite article is often omitted, unless *possibile* is added to the adverb:

Parla più chiaramente di tutti.	She speaks the most clearly of all.
Parliamo il più chiaramente possibile.	We're speaking as clearly as possible.

12. ABSOLUTE SUPERLATIVE

1. The absolute superlative is formed by dropping the last vowel of the adjective and adding *-issimo, -issima, -issimi, -issime:*

L'esercizio è facilissimo.	The exercise is very easy.

2. By putting the words *molto, troppo,* or *assai* in front of the adjectives:

La poesia è molto bella.	The poem is very beautiful.

3. By using a second adjective of almost the same meaning, or by repeating the adjective:

La casa è piena zeppa di amici.	The house is full of (loaded with) friends.
La macchina è nuova nuova.	The car is brand new.

4. By using *stra-, arci-, sopra-, super-, extra-:*

Il signore è straricco. (or) *Il signore è arciricco.*	The gentleman is loaded with money.
Questa seta è sopraffina.	This silk is extra fine.

13. IRREGULAR COMPARATIVES AND SUPERLATIVES

Some adjectives and adverbs have irregular comparatives and superlatives in addition to the regular forms.

ADJECTIVE	COMPARATIVE	SUPERLATIVE
good	better	the best
buono(a)	*più buono(a)*	*il più buono*
	migliore	*buonissimo(a)*
		ottimo(a)
		il/la migliore
bad	worse	the worst
cattivo(a)	*peggiore*	*il/la peggiore*
	più cattivo(a)	*il/la più cattivo(a)*
		pessimo(a)
		cattivissimo(a)
big/great	bigger/greater	the biggest/greatest
grande	*maggiore*	*il/la maggiore*
	più grande	*grandissimo(a)*
		il/la più grande
		massimo(a)
small/little	smaller/lesser	the smallest
piccolo(a)	*minore*	*il/la minore*
	più piccolo(a)	*il/la più piccolo(a)*
		piccolissimo(a)
		minimo(a)

ADVERB	COMPARATIVE	SUPERLATIVE
well	better	the best
bene	*meglio*	*il meglio*
badly	worse	the worst
male	*peggio*	*il peggio*

14. DIMINUTIVES AND AUGMENTATIVES

1. The endings *-ino, -ina, -ello, -ella, -etto, -etta, -uccio, -uccia* imply smallness:

cagnolino	puppy
gattino	kitty

2. The endings *-one, -ona, -otta* imply largeness:

omone	big man
stupidone	big fool

3. The endings *-ino, -uccio* indicate endearment:

tesoruccio	little treasure
caruccia	little darling

4. The endings *-accio, -accia, -astro, -astra, -azzo, -azza* indicate depreciation:

cagnaccio	ugly dog

15. Masculine and Feminine

Nouns referring to males are masculine; nouns referring to females are feminine:

il padre	the father	*la madre*	the mother
il figlio	the son	*la figlia*	the daughter
l'uomo	the man	*la donna*	the woman
il toro	the bull	*la vacca*	the cow
il gatto	the tomcat	*la gatta*	the female cat

MASCULINE NOUNS

1. Nouns ending in *-o* are usually masculine:

il corpo	the body
il cielo	the sky
il denaro	the money

2. The names of the months and the names of the days (except Sunday) are masculine:

il gennaio	January
il lunedì	Monday

3. The names of lakes and many names of mountains are masculine:

il Garda	Lake Garda
gli Appennini	the Apennines

FEMININE NOUNS

Nouns ending in *-a* are usually feminine:

la testa	the head
la città	the city
la quantità	the quantity

NOUNS ENDING IN *-E*

Nouns ending in *-e* in the singular may be either masculine or feminine:

la madre	the mother
il padre	the father
la legge	the law
il piede	the foot

NOUNS WITH MASCULINE AND FEMININE FORMS

1. Some masculine nouns ending in *-a, -e, -o* form their feminine in *-essa:*

il poeta	the poet	*la poetessa*	the poetess
il conte	the count	*la contessa*	the countess

2. Masculine nouns ending in -*tore* form their feminine in -*trice:*

l'attore	the actor	*l'attrice*	the actress

16. PLURALS OF NOUNS

1. Nouns ending in -*o,* mostly masculine, form their plural in -*i:*

il lupo	the wolf	*i lupi*	the wolves

SOME EXCEPTIONS

Some nouns ending in -*o* are feminine:

la mano	the hand	*le mani*	the hands
la radio	the radio	*le radio*	the radios
la dinamo	the dynamo	*le dinamo*	the dynamos

Some masculine nouns ending in -*o* have two plurals, with different meanings for each plural:

il braccio	the arm
i bracci	the arms (of a stream)
le braccia	the arms (of the body)

2. Nouns ending in -*a,* usually feminine, form their plural in -*e:*

la rosa	the rose	*le rose*	the roses

A number of masculine nouns ending in -*a* form their plural in -*i:*

il poeta	the poet	*i poeti*	the poets

3. Nouns ending in *-e,* which can be masculine or feminine, form their plural in *-i:*

il nipote	the nephew or grandson	*i nipoti*	the nephews or grandsons
la nipote	the niece or granddaughter	*le nipoti*	the nieces or granddaughters

SPECIAL CASES

1. Nouns ending in *-ca* or *-ga* insert *h* in the plural:

la barca	the boat	*le barche*	the boats
il monarca	the monarch	*i monarchi*	the monarchs

Exception:

un Belga	a Belgian	*i Belgi*	the Belgians

2. Nouns ending in *-cia* or *-gia* (with unaccented *i*) form their plural in *-ce* or *-ge* if the *c* or *g* is double or is preceded by another consonant:

la spiaggia	the seashore	*le spiagge*	the seashores
la guancia	the cheek	*le guance*	the cheeks

Nouns ending in *-cia* or *-gia* form their plural in *-cie* or *-gie* if *c* or *g* is preceded by a vowel or if the *i* is accented:

la fiducia	the trust	*le fiducie*	the trusts
le bugia	the lie	*le bugie*	the lies

3. Nouns ending in *-io* (without an accent on the *i*) have a single *i* in the plural:

il figlio	the son	*i figli*	the sons

If the *i* is accented, the plural has *ii:*

lo zio	the uncle	*gli zii*	the uncles

4. Nouns ending in *-co* or *-go* form their plural in *-chi* or *-ghi* if the accent falls on the syllable before the last:

il fico	the fig	*i fichi*	the figs

Exception:

l'amico	the friend	*gli amici*	the friends

If the accent falls on the second-to-last syllable, the plural is in *-ci* or *-gi:*

il medico	the doctor	*i medici*	the doctors

5. Nouns in the singular with the accent on the last vowel do not change in the plural:

la città	the city	*le città*	the cities

17. DAYS OF THE WEEK

The days of the week (except Sunday) are masculine and are not capitalized unless they begin a sentence. The article is only used when referring to a repeated, habitual event, as in "on Sundays" "on Mondays," etc.

lunedì	Monday
martedì	Tuesday
mercoledì	Wednesday
giovedì	Thursday
venerdì	Friday
sabato	Saturday
domenica	Sunday

Lunedì è il primo giorno della settimana.	Monday is the first day of the week.
Andranno a fare loro visita domenica.	They're going to pay them a visit on Sunday.
Domani è sabato.	Tomorrow is Saturday.
La domenica vado in chiesa.	On Sundays I go to church.
Vado a scuola il venerdì.	I go to school on Fridays.

Note: The word *on* is not translated before the days of the week or a date.

il 15 febbraio	on February 15

18. MONTHS OF THE YEAR

The names of the months are masculine and are not capitalized unless they begin a sentence. They are usually used without the definite article:

gennaio	January
febbraio	February
marzo	March
aprile	April
maggio	May
giugno	June
luglio	July
agosto	August
settembre	September
ottobre	October
novembre	November
dicembre	December

19. THE SEASONS

l'inverno (masc.)	winter
la primavera	spring
l'estate (fem.)	summer
l'autunno (masc.)	fall

The names of the seasons are usually not capitalized. They are preceded by the definite article, but after *di* the article may or may not be used:

L'inverno è una brutta stagione.	Winter is an ugly season.
Fa freddo d'inverno.	It's cold in (the) winter.
Io lavoro durante i mesi d'estate (or dell'estate).	I work during the summer months.

20. NUMBERS

The plural of *mille* (thousand) is *mila; duemila,* two thousand; *seimila,* six thousand.

After *milione* the preposition *di* is used:

un milione di soldati	one million soldiers
tre milioni di dollari	three million dollars

In writing a date, give the day first and then the month:

5 (cinque) agosto	August 5th
10 (dieci) novembre	November 10th

The ordinal numeral is used only for the first of the month:

il primo novembre	November 1st
il tre agosto	August 3rd

21. DEMONSTRATIVES

questo, -a, -i, -e	this, these
quello, -a, -i, -e	that, those

The pronoun "this" is *questo:*

Questo è l'uomo che cerchiamo.	This is the man we are looking for.

Besides the forms of *quello* already given, there are also the forms *quel, quei, quegli*. Here is how they are used:

1. If the article *il* is used before the noun, use *quel*:

il libro	the book
quel libro	that book

2. If *i* is used before the noun, use *quei*:

i maestri	the teachers
quei maestri	those teachers

3. If *gli* is used before the noun, use *quegli*:

gli studenti	the students
quegli studenti	those students

The same rules apply to *bel, bei, begli*, from *bello, -a, -i, -e*, "beautiful."

22. POSSESSIVE ADJECTIVES

Always use the article in front of a possessive adjective:

il mio denaro	my money
la tua sedia	your chair
la vostra borsa	your pocketbook

Except for members of the family in the singular:

mia madre	my mother

The possessive adjective agrees with the thing possessed and not with the possessor:

la sua chiave	(his, her) key

Suo may mean *his* or *her*, or, with the polite form, *your*. If confusion should arise because of the use of *suo*, use *di lui*, *di lei*, etc.

23. INDEFINITE ADJECTIVES

1. *qualche* (used only in *sing.*)   some
   alcuni (used only in *pl.*)   some

qualche lettera   some letters
alcuni dollari   some dollars

Note: *Alcuni* can be also used as a pronoun: *alcuni . . . altri* (some . . . others).

2. *qualunque, qualsiasi*   any
   (has no *pl.*)

qualunque mese   any month
qualsiasi ragazzo   any boy

3. *ogni* (has no *pl.*)   every or each
   ciascun, ciascuno,   each or every
   ciascuna (no *pl.*)

Ogni ragazzo parla.   Every boy talks.
Ogni ragazza parla.   Every girl talks.
Diciamo una parola a   Let's say a word to each
   ciascun signore.   gentlemen.
Raccontate tutto a   Tell everything to each
   ciascuna signora.   (or every) woman.

4. *altro (l' altro), altra, altri,*   other or more
   altre

Mandiamo gli altri libri?   Do we send the other
                                     books?

Vuole altro denaro?   Do you want more
                                     money?

5. *nessuno, nessun,*   no, no one
    nessuna

Nessuno zio ha scritto.   No uncle wrote.
Nessun soldato ha paura.   No soldier is afraid.
Nessuna sedia è buona.   No chair is good.

24. INDEFINITE PRONOUNS

1. *alcuni*   some
    alcuni . . . altri   some . . . some

alcuni dei suoi discorsi   some of his speeches
Di questi libri, alcuni sono   Of these books, some are
    buoni, altri cattivi.   good, some bad.

2. *qualcuno,*   someone, somebody
    qualcheduno
    (no *fem.*, no *pl.*)

Qualcuno è venuto.   Somebody came.
Qualcheduno ci chiama.   Somebody is calling us.

3. *chiunque*   anybody, any one
    (no *fem.*, no *pl.*)

Chiunque dice così.   Anybody says so.

4. *ognuno* (only *sing.*),   everybody, everyone
    tutti (only *pl.*)
    ciascuno (only   each or each one, everything
    sing.), *tutto*

Ognuno corre.   Everybody runs.
Tutti corrono.   Everybody runs. (All run.)

5. *l'altro, l'altra, gli altri, le altre, altro* — the other, the others; (in interrogative or negative sentences) else, anything else

un altro — another one

Lui dice una cosa ma l'altro non è d'accordo. — He says one thing, but the other one does not agree.

Volete altro? — Do you want something else?

Non vogliamo altro. — We do not want anything else.

6. *niente, nulla* — nothing
nessuno (no *fem.*, no *pl.*) — nobody, no one

Niente (nulla) lo consola. — Nothing consoles him.
Nessuno conosce questa regola. — Nobody knows this rule.

25. INTERROGATIVE PRONOUNS AND ADJECTIVES

1. The interrogative pronoun *chi* refers to persons, and corresponds to *who, whom,* or *which,* as illustrated by the three examples following:

Chi vi scrive? — Who writes to you?
Chi vediamo? — Whom do we see?
Chi di noi ha parlato? — Which one of us has talked?

2. *Che* or *che cosa* translates as *what:*

Che facciamo? — What are we doing?
Che cosa leggete? — What are you reading?

3. The two interrogative adjectives *quale* and *che* mean *which, what:*

Quale dei due giornali compra Lei?	Which of the two newspapers do you buy?
Che colore desiderate?	What color do you want?

26. RELATIVE PRONOUNS

chi	he who, him who
che	who, whom, that, which
cui	(used with prepositions)
a cui	to whom
di cui	of whom, of which
in cui	in which

Chi studia impara.	He who studies, learns.
l'uomo che ho visto	the man whom I saw
la donna di cui parlo	the woman of whom I speak
la ragazza a cui parlo	the girl to whom I'm speaking

1. *che* (undeclinable): For masculine, feminine, singular, plural; for persons, animals, things. Do not use this pronoun if there is a preposition.

2. *il quale, la quale, i quali, le quali:* For persons, animals, things, with the same English meanings as *che;* can be used with or without prepositions. When used with prepositions, the contracted forms are used, e.g., *alla quale, dei quali,* etc.

3. *cui* (undeclinable): Masculine, feminine, singular, plural; for persons, animals, things; is always used with a preposition.

27. PERSONAL PRONOUNS

Pronouns have different forms depending on whether they are:

1. The subject of a verb
2. The direct object of a verb
3. The indirect object of a verb
4. Used after a preposition
5. Used with reflexive verbs

a. The subject pronouns are:

SINGULAR

io	I
tu	you *(fam.)*
lui	he
lei	she
Lei	you *(pol.)*
esso	it *(masc.)*
essa	it *(fem.)*

PLURAL

noi	we
voi	you
loro	they
Loro	you *(formal plur.)*

It is not necessary to use subject pronouns as the verb ending indicates who is speaking or being spoken about.

b. The direct object pronouns are:

mi	me
ti	you *(fam.)*
lo	him, it
la	her, it, you *(pol.)*
ci	us
vi	you
li	them, you
le	them, you

Ci vede.	He sees us.
Lo scrive.	He writes it.

c. The indirect object pronouns are:

mi	to me
ti	to you *(fam.)*
gli	to him
le	to her
Le	to you *(pol.)*
ci	to us
vi	to you
loro	to them, to you *(form.)*

Lui mi scrive una lettera.	He is writing me a letter.
Io ti regalo una bambola.	I am giving you a doll.
Noi parliamo loro.	We speak to them.

d. The pronouns used after a preposition are:

me	me
te	you *(fam.)*
lui	him
lei	her, you *(pol.)*
noi	us
voi	you
loro	them, you *(form.)*

Io verrò con te.	I will come with you.
Lui parla sempre di lei.	He always speaks about her.

e. The reflexive pronouns are:

mi	myself
ti	yourself *(fam.)*
si	himself, herself, itself, yourself *(pol.)*

ci	ourselves
vi	yourselves
si	themselves, yourselves *(form.)*

Io mi lavo.	I wash myself.
Noi ci alziamo alle nove.	We get up at nine.
Loro si alzano.	They get up.

28. POSITION OF PRONOUNS

1. Pronouns are written as separate words, except with the imperative, infinitive, and gerund, where they follow the verbal form and are written as one word with it:

Ditelo.	Say it.
Fatemi un favore.	Do me a favor.
facendolo . . .	doing it . . .
chiamandolo	calling him
scriverle una lettera	to write her a letter
dopo avermi chiamato	after having called me

2. In the imperative, when the polite form is used, the pronouns are never attached to the verb:

Mi faccia un favore.	Do me a favor.

3. Some verbs of one syllable in the imperative double the initial consonant of the pronoun:

Dimmi una cosa.	Tell me one thing.
Facci una cortesia.	Do us a favor.

4. In the compound infinitive the pronoun is generally attached to the auxiliary:

Credo di averti dato tutto.	I think I gave you everything.

The simple infinitive drops the final *e* before the pronoun:

leggere un articolo	to read an article
leggerti un articolo	to read you an article

5. When two object pronouns are used with the same verb, the indirect precedes the direct:

Te lo voglio dire.	I want to tell it to you.

Observe the following changes in the pronouns that occur in this case:

The *i* in *mi, ti, ci, vi, si* changes to *e* before *lo, la, le, li, ne,* while *gli* takes an additional *e* and is written as one word with the following pronoun. *Le* also becomes *glie* before *lo, la, li, le, ne:*

Ce lo dà.	He gives it to us.
Glielo mando a casa.	I send it to him (to her, to you) at home.
Glielo dicono.	They tell it to him (to her, to you).

29. NE

1. Used as a pronoun meaning *of him, of her, of them, of it:*

Parla del mio amico?	Are you talking of my friend?
Sì ne parlo.	Yes, I am talking of him.
Parliamo noi di questa cosa?	Are we talking of this thing?
Sì, ne parliamo.	Yes, we are talking of it.

2. Used as a partitive meaning "some" or "any":

Mangia la signorina del pesce?	Does the young lady eat some fish?
Sì, ne mangia.	Yes, she does (eat some).

3. Used as an adverb of place, meaning *from* or *out of:*

Gli studenti escono dalla classe?	Are the students coming out from the class?
Sì, ne escono.	Yes, they are (coming out).

30. *Si*

1. *Si* can be used as a reflexive pronoun:

Lui si lava.	He washes himself.
Loro si lavano.	They wash themselves.

2. *Si* is used as an impersonal pronoun:

Non sempre si riflette su quel che si dice.	Not always does one ponder over what one says.
Qui si mangia bene.	Here one eats well.

3. *Si* is sometimes used to translate the English passive:

Come si manda questa lettera?	How is this letter sent?

31. ADVERBS

1. Many adverbs end in *-mente:*

caramente	dearly
dolcemente	sweetly

These adverbs are easily formed; take the feminine, singular form of the adjective and add *-mente*. For instance, "dear" = *caro, cara, cari, care;* the feminine singular is *cara*, and so the adverb will be *caramente*. "Sweet" is *dolce, dolci* (there is no difference between the masculine and feminine); the feminine singular is *dolce*, and so the adverb will be *dolcemente*.

2. Adjectives ending in *-le* or *-re* drop the final *e* before *-mente* if the *l* or *r* is preceded by a vowel; thus the adverb corresponding to *facile* is *facilmente* (easily); *celere* (fast) becomes *celermente* (fast, *adv.*). The adverbs corresponding to *buono* (good) and *cattivo* (bad) are *bene* and *male*.

3. Adverbs may have a comparative and superlative form: *Caramente, più caramente, molto caramente,* or *carissimamente*.

Observe these irregular comparative and superlative forms of adverbs:

meglio	better
peggio	worse
maggiormente	more greatly
massimamente	very greatly
minimamente	in the least
ottimamente	very well
pessimamente	very bad

32. PREPOSITIONS

1. The most common prepositions in Italian are:

di	of
a	at, to
da	from
in	in
con	with
su, sopra	above
per	through, by means of, on
tra, fra	between, among

2. When used before a definite article, these prepositions are often contracted. Here are the most common of these combinations:

di + il = del	*a + il = al*
di + lo = dello	*a + lo = allo*
di + la = della	*a + la = alla*
di + l' = dell'	*a + l' = all'*
di + i = dei	*a + i = ai*
di + gli = degli	*a + gli = agli*
di + le = delle	*a + le = alle*
con + il = col	*sul + il = sul*
con + i = coi	*su + la = sulla*
	su + lo = sullo
	su + gli = sugli
	su + i = sui

Io ho del denaro.	I have some money.
il cavallo dello zio	the uncle's horse
Io regalo un dollaro al ragazzo.	I give a dollar to the boy.
Il professore risponde agli studenti.	The professor answers the students.

33. NEGATION

1. *Non* (not) comes before the verb:

Io non vedo.	I don't see.
Lui non parla.	He isn't speaking.

2. Nothing, never, no one:

Non vedo nulla.	I see nothing.
Non vado mai.	I never go.
Non viene nessuno.	No one comes.

If the negative pronoun begins the sentence, *non* is not used.

Nessuno viene.	No one comes.

34. QUESTION WORDS

Che?	What?
Che cosa?	What?
Perchè?	Why?
Come?	How?
Quanto?	How much?
Quando?	When?
Dove?	Where?
Quale?	Which?

35. THE TENSES OF VERBS

Italian verbs are divided into three classes (conjugations) according to their infinitives:

Class I—*parlare, amare*
Class II—*scrivere, temere*
Class III—*partire, sentire*

1. The present:
   To form the present tense, take off the infinitive ending (*-are, -ere, -ire*) and add the following present tense endings:

FIRST CONJ. (I)	SECOND CONJ. (II)	THIRD CONJ. (III)
-o	*-o*	*-o*
-i	*-i*	*-i*
-a	*-e*	*-e*
-iamo	*-iamo*	*-iamo*
-ate	*-ete*	*-ite*
-ano	*-ono*	*-ono*

The present tense can be translated in several ways:

Io parlo italiano.   I speak Italian. I am speaking
                                   Italian. I do speak Italian.

2. The imperfect:

I	II	III
-avo	*-evo*	*-ivo*
-avi	*-evi*	*-ivi*
-ava	*-eva*	*-iva*
-avamo	*-evamo*	*-ivamo*
-avate	*-evate*	*-ivate*
-avano	*-evano*	*-ivano*

The imperfect is used:

a. To indicate continued or customary action in the past:

Quando ero a Roma andavo sempre a visitare i musei.	When I was in Rome, I was always visiting the museums.
Lo incontravo ogni giorno.	I used to meet him every day.

b. To indicate what was happening when something else happened:

Lui scriveva quando lei entrò.	He was writing when she entered.

3. The future:
The future of regular verbs is formed by adding to the infinitive (after the final *e* is dropped) the endings *-ò; -ai; -à; -emo; -ete; -anno*. For the first conjugation, the *a* of the infinitive changes to *e*.

The future generally expresses actions that will take place in the future:

Lo comprerò.	I'll buy it.
Andrò domani.	I'll go tomorrow.

Sometimes it expresses probability or conjecture:

Che ora sarà?	What time can it be? What time do you think it must be?
Sarà l'una.	It must be one.
Starà mangiando ora.	He's probably eating now.

4. *Passato remoto* (preterit, past definite):
   This tense indicates an action that happened in a period of time completely finished now. Although there are some regions in Italy where the *passato remoto* is used in conversation, it is chiefly a literary tense, and the *passato prossimo* is used in conversation instead.

Romolo fondò Roma.	Romulus founded Rome.
Dante nacque nel 1265.	Dante was born in 1265.
Garibaldi combattè per l'unità d'Italia.	Garibaldi fought for the unity of Italy.

5. *Passato prossimo* (compound past):
   The *passato prossimo* is formed by adding the past participle to the present indicative of *avere* or *essere*. It is used to indicate a past action and corresponds to the English preterit or present perfect:

Io ho finito il mio lavoro.	I finished my work. (I have finished my work.)
L'hai visto?	Have you seen him?
Sono arrivati.	They arrived.

6. The past perfect tense is formed by adding the past participle to the imperfect of *avere* or *essere*.

Lui l'aveva fatto.	He had done it.

7. The *trapassato remoto* (preterit perfect) is formed by adding the past participle to the past definite of *avere*

or *essere*. It is a literary tense used to indicate an event that had happened just before another event:

Quando uscì ebbe finito.   When he went out, he had
                                finished.

8. The future perfect tense is formed by adding the past participle to the future of *avere* or *essere*.

Lui avrà finito presto.   He will soon have finished.

The future perfect can also be used to indicate probability:

Lui sarà stato ammalato.   He was probably sick.
Saranno già partiti.   They probably left already.

Complete conjugation of a sample verb from each class:

AMARE (FIRST CONJUGATION): TO LOVE, TO LIKE

INDICATIVE

PRESENT
io amo
tu ami
lui/lei/Lei ama
noi amiamo
voi amate
loro amano

IMPERFECT
io amavo
tu amavi
lui/lei/Lei amava
noi amavamo
voi amavate
loro amavano

FUTURE
io amerò
tu amerai
lui/lei/Lei amerà
noi ameremo
voi amerete
loro ameranno

PRESENT PERFECT
io ho amato
tu hai amato
lui/lei/Lei ha amato
noi abbiamo amato
voi avete amato
loro hanno amato

PRETERIT

io amai
tu amasti
lui/lei/Lei amò
noi amammo
voi amaste
loro amarono

PAST PERFECT

io avevo amato
tu avevi amato
lui/lei/Lei aveva amato
noi avevamo amato
voi avevate amato
loro avevano amato

PRETERIT PERFECT

io ebbi amato
tu avesti amato
lui/lei/Lei ebbe amato
noi avemmo amato
voi aveste amato
loro ebbero amato .

FUTURE PERFECT

io avrò amato
tu avrai amato
lui/lei/Lei avrà amato
noi avremo amato
voi avrete amato
loro avranno amato

SUBJUNCTIVE

PRESENT

che io ami
che tu ami
che lui/lei/Lei ami
che noi amiamo
che voi amiate
che loro amino

IMPERFECT

che io amassi
che tu amassi
che lui/lei/Lei amasse
che noi amassimo
che voi amaste
che loro amassero

PERFECT

che io abbia amato
che tu abbia amato
che lui/lei/Lei abbia amato
che noi abbiamo amato
che voi abbiate amato
che lui abbiano amato

PAST PERFECT

che io avessi amato
che tu avessi amato
che lui/lei/Lei avesse amato
che noi avessimo amato
che voi aveste amato
che loro avessero amato

IMPERATIVE

PRESENT
ama (tu)
ami (Lei)
amiamo (noi)
amate (voi)
amino (Loro)

CONDITIONAL

PRESENT	PERFECT
io amerei	*io avrei amato*
tu ameresti	*tu avresti amato*
lui/lei/Lei amerebbe	*lui/lei/Lei avrebbe amato*
noi ameremmo	*noi avremmo amato*
voi amereste	*voi avreste amato*
loro amerebbero	*loro avrebbero amato*

INFINITIVES

PRESENT	PERFECT
amare	*avere amato*

PARTICIPLES

PRESENT	PERFECT
amante	*amato*

GERUNDS

PRESENT	PERFECT
amando	*avendo amato*

TEMERE (SECOND CONJUGATION): TO FEAR

INDICATIVE

PRESENT	IMPERFECT
io temo	*io temevo*
tu temi	*tu temevi*
lui/lei/Lei teme	*lui/lei/Lei temeva*
noi temiamo	*noi temevamo*
voi temete	*voi temevate*
loro temono	*loro temevano*

FUTURE	PRESENT PERFECT
io temerò	*io ho temuto*
tu temerai	*tu hai temuto*
lui/lei/Lei temerà	*lui/lei/Lei ha temuto*
noi temeremo	*noi abbiamo temuto*
voi temerete	*voi avete temuto*
loro temeranno	*loro hanno temuto*

PRETERIT	PAST PERFECT
io temei (or -etti)	*io avevo temuto*
tu temesti	*tu avevi temuto*
lui/lei/Lei temè (or -ette)	*lui/lei/Lei aveva temuto*
noi tememmo	*noi avevamo temuto*
voi temeste	*voi avevate temuto*
loro temerono (or -ettero)	*loro avevano temuto*

PRETERIT PERFECT	FUTURE PERFECT
io ebbi temuto	*io avrò temuto*
tu avesti temuto	*tu avrai temuto*
lui/lei/Lei ebbe temuto	*lui/lei/Lei avrà temuto*
noi avemmo temuto	*noi avremo temuto*
voi aveste temuto	*voi avrete temuto*
loro ebbero temuto	*loro avranno temuto*

SUBJUNCTIVE

PRESENT	IMPERFECT
che io tema	*che io temessi*
che tu tema	*che tu temessi*
che lui/lei/Lei tema	*che lui/lei/Lei temesse*
che noi temiamo	*che noi temessimo*
che voi temiate	*che voi temeste*
che loro temano	*che loro temessero*

PERFECT	PAST PERFECT
che io abbia temuto	*che io avessi temuto*
che tu abbia temuto	*che tu avessi temuto*
che lui/lei/Lei abbia temuto	*che lui/lei/Lei avesse temuto*

che noi abbiamo temuto

che noi avessimo temuto

che voi abbiate temuto

che voi aveste temuto

che loro abbiano temuto

che loro avessero temuto

IMPERATIVE

PRESENT

temi (tu)

tema (Lei)

temiamo (noi)

temete (voi)

temano (Loro)

CONDITIONAL

PRESENT

io temerei

tu temeresti

lui/lei/Lei temerebbe

noi temeremmo

voi temereste

loro temerebbero

PERFECT

io avrei temuto

tu avresti temuto

lui/lei/Lei avrebbe temuto

noi avremmo temuto

voi avreste temuto

loro avrebbero temuto

INFINITIVES

PRESENT

temere

PERFECT

aver temuto

PARTICIPLES

PRESENT

temente

PERFECT

temuto

GERUNDS

PRESENT

temendo

PERFECT

avendo temuto

SENTIRE (THIRD CONJUGATION): TO HEAR

INDICATIVE

PRESENT
io sento
tu senti
lui/lei/Lei sente
noi sentiamo
voi sentite
loro sentono

IMPERFECT
io sentivo
tu sentivi
lui/lei/Lei sentiva
noi sentivamo
voi sentivate
loro sentivano

FUTURE
io sentirò
tu sentirai
lui/lei/Lei sentirà
noi sentiremo
voi sentirete
loro sentiranno

PRESENT PERFECT
io ho sentito
tu hai sentito
lui/lei/Lei ha sentito
noi avevamo sentito
voi avete sentito
loro hanno sentito

PRETERIT
io sentii
tu sentisti
lui/lei/Lei sentì
noi sentimmo
voi sentiste
loro sentirono

PAST PERFECT
io avevo sentito
tu avevi sentito
lui/lei/Lei aveva sentito
noi avevamo sentito
voi avevate sentito
loro avevano sentito

PRETERIT PERFECT
io ebbi sentito
tu avesti sentito
lui/lei/Lei ebbe sentito
noi avemmo sentito
voi aveste sentito
loro ebbero sentito

FUTURE PERFECT
io avrò sentito
tu avrai sentito
lui/lei/Lei avrà sentito
noi avremo sentito
voi avrete sentito
loro avranno sentito

SUBJUNCTIVE

PRESENT
che io senta
che tu senta
che lui/lei/Lei senta
che noi sentiamo
che voi sentiate
che loro sentano

IMPERFECT
che io sentissi
che tu sentissi
che lui/lei/Lei sentisse
che noi sentissimo
che voi sentiste
che loro sentissero

PERFECT
che io abbia sentito
che tu abbia sentito
che lui/lei/Lei abbia sentito
che noi abbiamo sentito
che voi abbiate sentito
che loro abbiano sentito

PAST PERFECT
che io avessi sentito
che tu avessi sentito
che lui/lei/Lei avesse sentito
che noi avessimo sentito
che voi aveste sentito
che loro avessero sentito

IMPERATIVE

PRESENT
senti (tu)
senta (Lei)
sentiamo (noi)
sentite (voi)
sentano (Loro)

CONDITIONAL

PRESENT
io sentirei
tu sentiresti
lui/lei/Lei sentirebbe
noi sentiremmo
voi sentireste
loro sentirebbero

PERFECT
io avrei sentito
tu avresti sentito
lui/lei/Lei avrebbe sentito
noi avremmo sentito
voi avreste sentito
loro avrebbero sentito

INFINITIVES

PRESENT	PERFECT
sentire	*aver sentito*

PARTICIPLES

PRESENT	PERFECT
sentente	*sentito*

GERUNDS

PRESENT	PERFECT
sentendo	*avendo sentito*

36. THE PAST PARTICIPLE

1. The past participle ends in:

-ato, (-ata, -ati, -ate)   *parl -ato*
   (for the First Conjugation)

-uto   *bev -uto*
   (for the Second Conjugation)

-ito   *part -ito*
   (for the Third Conjugation)

2. The past participle used with *essere* agrees with the subject of the verb:

è andato	he left
sono andate	they *(fem.)* left

3. The past participle used with *avere* generally agrees with the preceding direct object pronoun:

Ho comprato i libri.	I bought the books.
Li ho comprati.	I bought them.

Ho visto Anna. I saw Anna.
L'ho vista. I saw her.

37. USE OF THE AUXILIARIES

The most common intransitive verbs that are conjugated with the verb *essere* in the compound tenses are the following:

andare, arrivare, scendere, entrare, salire, morire, nascere, partire, restare, ritornare, uscire, cadere, venire, rivenire.

Io sono venuto (-a). I have come.
Lui è arrivato. He has arrived.
Noi siamo partiti. We have left.

Reflexive verbs form their compound tenses with *essere*. If there is a direct object, the past participle generally agrees with it, and not with the subject:

La signorina si è rotto il braccio. The young lady broke her arm.

The past tenses of passive constructions are formed with *essere:*

Il ragazzo è amato. The boy is loved.
La ragazza è stata amata. The girl has been loved.
I ragazzi furono amati. The boys were loved.
Le ragazze saranno amate. The girls will be loved.

Sometimes the verb *venire* is used instead of *essere* in a passive construction:

La poesia è letta dal maestro. The poem is read by the teacher.
La poesia viene letta dal maestro. The poem is read by the teacher.

38. The Present Progressive

Io fumo means "I smoke" or "I am smoking," but there is also a special way of translating "I am smoking": *Io sto fumando*. In other words, Italian uses the verb *stare* with the present gerund of the main verb to emphasize that an action is in progress:

Noi stiamo leggendo.	We are reading.
Lui stava scrivendo.	He was writing.

This form is generally used only in the simple tenses.

39. The Subjunctive

Formation

1. The present tense

   a. First Conjugation: by dropping the *-are* from the infinitive and adding *-i, -i, -i, -iamo, -iate, -ino*.

Penso che lui parli troppo.	I think (that) he speaks too much.

   b. Second and Third Conjugations: by dropping the *-ere* and *-ire* and adding *-a, -a, -a, -iamo, -iate, -iano*.

Sebbene Lei scriva in fretta non fa errori.	Although you write fast, you make no mistakes.

2. The imperfect tense

   a. First Conjugation: by dropping the *-are* and adding *-assi, -assi, -asse, -assimo, -aste, -assero*.

Credevo che il ragazzo lavorasse molto.	I thought (that) the boy was working hard.

b. Second Conjugation: by dropping the *-ere* and adding *-essi, -essi, -esse, -essimo, -este, -essero*.

Prima che le signorina scrivesse la lettera il padre la chiamò.	Before the girl could write the letter, her father called her.

c. Third Conjugation: by dropping the *-ire* and adding *-issi, -issi, -isse, -issimo, -iste, -issero*.

Ero del parere che il mio amico si sentisse male.	I was under the impression that my friend did not feel well.

3. The compound tenses (perfect and past perfect)
These are formed with the present and imperfect of the subjunctive of "to have" and "to be" and the past participle.

Credo che gli studenti abbiano finito la lezione.	I think (that) the students have finished the lesson.
Era possibile che i mei amici fossero già arrivati in città.	It was possible that my friends had already arrived in town.

Uses of the Subjunctive

The subjunctive mood expresses doubt, uncertainty, hope, fear, desire, supposition, possibility, probability, granting, etc. For this reason, it is mostly found in clauses dependent upon another verb.

1. In a few cases the subjunctive is used alone. The most common one is when expressing a wish or desire:

Siate felici!	May you be happy!

2. The subjunctive is used in dependent clauses in the following ways:

a. After verbs expressing hope, wish, desire, command, doubt:

Voglio che tu ci vada.　　　　I want you to go there.

b. After verbs expressing an opinion *(penso, credo)*:

Penso che sia vero.　　　　I think it is true.

c. After expressions made with a form of *essere* and an adjective or an adverb *(è necessario, è facile, è possibile)*, or some impersonal expressions like *bisogna, importa,* etc.:

È necessario che io parta　　It is necessary that I leave
　subito.　　　　　　　　immediately.
È impossibile che noi　　　It is impossible for us to come
　veniamo questa sera.　　this evening.

d. After some conjunctions—*sebbene, quantunque, per quanto, benchè, affinchè, prima che* (subjunctive to express a possibility; indicative to express a fact):

Sebbene non sia guarito,　　Although I am not well yet,
　devo uscire.　　　　　　I must go out.
Benche io te l'abbia già　　Although I told you already,
　detto, ricordati di　　　remember to go to the Post
　andare alla Posta.　　　Office.

40. THE CONDITIONAL

The conditional is formed:

1. In the present tense:

a. First and Second Conjugations: by dropping the *-are,* or *-ere* and adding *-erei, -ereste, -erebbe, -eremmo, -ereste, -erebbero.*

La signora parlerebbe molto, se potesse.	The lady would speak a lot if she could.

b. Third Conjugation: by dropping the *-ire* and adding *-irei, -iresti, -irebbe, -iremmo, -ireste, -irebbero.*

Il signore si sentirebbe bene, se prendesse le pillole.	The gentleman would feel well if he took the pills.

2. In the past tense:
By using the present conditional of "to have" or "to be" and the past participle.

Mio cugino non avrebbe investito il suo denaro in questo, se l' avesse saputo primo.	My cousin would not have invested his money in this if he had known it before.

41. "IF" CLAUSES

An "if" clause can express:

1. *Reality.* In this case the indicative is used:

Se oggi pioverà, non uscirò.	If it rains today, I won't go out.

2. *Possibility.* The imperfect subjunctive and the conditional present are used to express possibility in the present:

Se tu leggessi, impareresti.	If you read, you would learn. (The idea is that it is possible that you may read and so you may learn.)

The past perfect subjunctive and the past conditional are used to express a possibility in the past:

Se tu avessi letto avresti imparato.	If you had read, you would have learned. (The idea is that you might have read and so might have learned.)

3. *Impossibility* or *unreality*. Use the same construction as in number 2; the only difference is that we know that the condition cannot be fulfilled.

Se l'uomo vivesse mille anni, imparerebbe molte cose.	If a man lived 1,000 years, he would learn many things. (But it's a fact that people don't live 1,000 years, and so don't learn many things.)
Se io avessi studiato quando ero giovane, avrei fatto un gran piacere ai miei genitori.	If I had studied when I was young, I would have given great pleasure to my parents. (But it's a fact that I did not study, and so I did not bring great pleasure to my parents.)

42. THE IMPERATIVE

The forms of the imperative are normally taken from the present indicative:

leggi	read *(familiar)*
leggiamo	let's read
leggete	read *(plural)*

For the First Conjugation, however, note:

canta	sing

The polite forms of the imperative are taken from the present subjunctive:

canti	sing
cantino	sing
legga	read
leggano	read

43. "To Be" and "To Have"

Essere and *avere,* "to be" and "to have," are very irregular. For your convenience, here are their complete conjugations.

ESSERE: TO BE

INDICATIVE

PRESENT
io sono
tu sei
lui/lei/Lei è
noi siamo
voi siete
loro sono

IMPERFECT
io ero
tu eri
lui/lei/Lei era
noi eravamo
voi eravate
loro erano

FUTURE
io sarò
tu sarai
lui/lei/Lei sarà
noi saremo
voi sarete
loro saranno

PRETERIT
io fui
tu fosti
lui/lei/Lei fu
noi fummo
voi foste
loro furono

PAST PERFECT
io ero stato/a
tu eri stato/a
lui/lei/Lei era stato/a
noi eravamo stati/e
voi eravate stati/e
loro erano stati/e

PRETERIT PERFECT
io fui stato/a
tu fosti stato/a
lui/lei/Lei fu stato/a
noi fummo stati/e
voi foste stati/e
loro furono stati/e

PRESENT PERFECT

io sono stato/a
tu sei stato/a
lui/lei/Lei è stato
noi siamo stati/e
voi siete stati/e
loro sono stati/e

FUTURE PERFECT

io sarò stato/a
tu sarai stato/a
lui/lei/Lei sarà stato
noi saremo stati/e
voi sarete stati/e
loro saranno stati/e

SUBJUNCTIVE

PRESENT

che io sia
che tu sia
che lui/lei/Lei sia
che noi siamo
che voi siate
che loro siano

IMPERFECT

che io fossi
che tu fossi
che lui/lei/Lei fosse
che noi fossimo
che voi foste
che loro fossero

PERFECT

che io sia stato/a
che tu sia stato/a
che lui/lei/Lei sia stato
che noi siamo stati/e
che voi siate stati/e
che loro siano stati/e

PAST PERFECT

che io fossi stato/a
che tu fossi stato/a
che lui/lei/Lei fosse stato/a
che noi fossimo stati/e
che voi foste stati/e
che loro fossero stati/e

IMPERATIVE

PRESENT

sii (tu)
sia (Lei)
siamo (noi)
siate (voi)
siano (Loro)

CONDITIONAL

PRESENT

io sarei
tu saresti

PERFECT

io sarei stato/a
tu saresti stato/a

lui/lei/Lei sarebbe
noi saremmo
voi sareste
loro sarebbero

lui/lei/Lei sarebbe stato/a
noi saremmo stati/e
voi sareste stati/e
loro sarebbero stati/e

INFINITIVE

PRESENT
essere

PERFECT
essere stato/a/i/e

PARTICIPLE

PERFECT
stato/a/i/e

GERUND

PRESENT
essendo

PERFECT
essendo stato/a/i/e

AVERE: TO HAVE

INDICATIVE

PRESENT
io ho
tu hai
lui/lei/Lei ha
noi abbiamo
voi avete
loro hanno

PRETERIT
io ebbi
tu avesti
lui/lei/Lei ebbe
noi avemmo
voi aveste
loro ebbero

IMPERFECT
io avevo
tu avevi
lui/lei/Lei aveva
noi avevamo
voi avevate
loro avevano

PAST PERFECT
io avevo avuto
tu avevi avuto
lui/lei/Lei aveva avuto
noi avevamo avuto
voi avevate avuto
loro avevano avuto

FUTURE
io avrò
tu avrai
lui/lei/Lei avrà
noi avremo
voi avrete
loro avranno

PRETERIT PERFECT
io ebbi avuto
tu avesti avuto
lui/lei/Lei ebbi avuto
noi avemmo avuto
voi aveste avuto
loro ebbero avuto

PRESENT PERFECT
io ho avuto
tu hai avuto
lui/lei/Lei ha avuto
noi abbiamo avuto
voi avete avuto
loro hanno avuto

FUTURE PERFECT
io avrò avuto
tu avrai avuto
lui/lei/Lei avrà avuto
noi avremo avuto
voi avrete avuto
loro avranno avuto

SUBJUNCTIVE

PRESENT
che io abbia
che tu abbia
che lui/lei/Lei abbia
che noi abbiamo
che voi abbiate
che loro abbiano

IMPERFECT
che io avessi
che tu avessi
che lui/lei/Lei avesse
che noi avessimo
che voi aveste
che loro avessero

PERFECT
che io abbia avuto
che tu abbia avuto
che lui/lei/Lei abbia avuto
che noi abbiamo avuto
che voi abbiate avuto
che loro abbiano avuto

PAST PERFECT
che io avessi avuto
che tu avessi avuto
che lui/lei/Lei avesse avuto
che noi avessimo avuto
che voi aveste avuto
che loro avessero avuto

IMPERATIVE

PRESENT
abbi (tu)
abbia (Lei)
abbiamo (noi)
abbiate (voi)
abbiano (Loro)

CONDITIONAL

PRESENT
io avrei
tu avresti
lui/lei/Lei avrebbe
noi avremmo
voi avreste
loro avrebbero

PERFECT
io avrei avuto
tu avresti avuto
lui/lei/Lei avrebbe avuto
noi avremmo avuto
voi avreste avuto
loro avrebbero avuto

INFINITIVE

PRESENT
avere

PERFECT
avere avuto

PARTICIPLES

PRESENT
avente

PERFECT
avuto

GERUND

PRESENT
avendo

PERFECT
avendo avuto

44. SOME IRREGULAR VERBS

(Only irregular tenses are indicated. Other tenses follow the regular pattern of the conjugation as shown in the tenses of the verb.)

Andare = to go
Ind. pres.: *vado, vai, va, andiamo, andate, vanno.*
Future: *andrò, andrai, andrà, andremo, andrete, andranno.*
Subj. pres.: *vada, vada, vada, andiamo, andiate, vadano.*

Imperative: *va', vada, andiamo, andate, vadano.*
Cond. pres.: *andrei, andresti, andrebbe, andremmo, andreste, andrebbero.*

Bere = to drink
Ind. pres.: *bevo, bevi, beve, beviamo, bevete, bevono.*
Imperfect: *bevevo, bevevi,* etc.
Preterit: *bevvi, bevesti, bevve, bevemmo, beveste, bevvero.*
Future: *berrò, berrai, berra, berremo, berrete, berrano.*
Subj. imp.: *bevessi, bevessi, bevesse, bevessimo, beveste, bevessero.*
Cond. pres.: *berrei, berresti, berrebbe, berremmo, berreste, berrebbero.*
Past part.: *bevuto.*

Cadere = to fall
Future: *cadrò, cadrai, cadrà, cadremo, cadrete, cadranno.*
Preterit: *caddi, cadesti, cadde, cademmo, cadeste, caddero.*
Cond. pres.: *cadrei, cadresti, cadrebbe, cadremmo, cadreste, cadrebbero.*

Chiedere = to ask
Preterit: *chiesi, chiedesti, chiese, chiedemmo, chiedeste, chiesero.*
Past part.: *chiesto.*

Chiudere = to shut
Preterit: *chiusi, chiudesti, chiuse, chiudemmo, chiudeste, chiusero.*
Past part.: *chiuso.*

Conoscere = to know
Preterit: *conobbi, conoscesti, conobbe, conoscemmo, conosceste, conobbero.*
Past part.: *conosciuto.*

Cuocere = to cook
Ind. pres.: *cuocio, cuoci, cuoce, cociamo, cocete, cuociono.*
Preterit: *cossi, cocesti, cosse, cocemmo, coceste, cossero.*
Subj. pres.: *cuocia* or *cuoca, cuocia/cuoca, cuocia/cuoca, c(u)ociamo, c(u)ociate, cuociano.*
Imperative: *cuoci, cuoc(i)a, c(u)ociamo, c(u)ociete, cuoc(i)ano.*
Past part.: *cotto.*

Dare = to give
Ind. pres.: *do, dai, dà, diamo, date, danno.*
Preterit: *diedi* or *detti, desti, diede* or *dette, demmo, deste, dettero* or *diedero.*
Subj. pres.: *dia, dia, dia, diamo, diate, diano.*
Subj. imper.: *dessi, dessi, desse, dessimo, deste, dessero.*
Imperative: *da', dia, diamo, date, diano.*
Past part.: *dato.*

Dire = to say
Ind. pres.: *dico, dici, dice, diciamo, dite, dicono.*
Imperfect: *dicevo, dicevi, diceva, dicevamo, dicevate, dicevano.*
Preterit: *dissi, dicesti, disse, dicemmo, diceste, dissero.*
Subj. pres.: *dica, dica, dica, diciamo, diciate, dicano.*
Subj. imper.: *dicessi, dicessi, dicesse, dicessimo, diceste, dicessero.*
Imperative: *di, dica, diciamo, dite, dicano.*
Past part.: *detto.*

Dolere = to suffer, to ache
Ind. pres.: *dolgo, duoli, duole, doliamo, dolete, dolgono.*
Preterit: *dolsi, dolesti, dolse, dolemmo, doleste, dolsero.*
Future: *dorrò, dorrai, dorrà, dorremo, dorrete, dorranno.*
Subj. pres.: *dolga,* etc., *doliamo, doliate, dolgano.*
Cond. pres.: *dorrei, dorresti, dorrebbe, dorremmo, dorreste, dorrebbero.*

Dovere = to owe, to be obliged

Ind. pres.: *devo* or *debbo, devi, deve, dobbiamo,* or *dovete, devono,* or *debbono.*

Future: *dovrò, dovrai, dovrà, dovremo, dovrete, dovranno.*

Subj. pres.: *deva* or *debba, deva* or *debba, deva* or *debba, dobbiamo, dobbiate, devano* or *debbano.*

Cond. pres.: *dovrei, dovresti, dovrebbe, dovremmo, dovreste, dovrebbero.*

Fare = to do

Ind. pres.: *faccio, fai, fa, facciamo, fate, fanno.*

Imperfect: *facevo, facevi, faceva, facevamo, facevate, facevano.*

Preterit: *feci, facesti, fece, facemmo, faceste, fecero.*

Subj. pres.: *faccia, faccia, faccia, facciamo, facciate, facciano.*

Subj. imp.: *facessi, facessi, facesse, facessimo, faceste, facessero.*

Imper. pres.: *fa', faccia, facciamo, fate, facciano.*

Past part.: *fatto.*

Godere = to enjoy

Future: *goderò* or *godrò, godrai, godrà, godremo, godrete, godranno.*

Cond. pres.: *godrei, godresti, godrebbe, godremmo, godreste, godrebbero.*

Leggere = to read

Preterit: *lessi, leggesti, lesse, leggemo, leggeste, lessero.*

Past part.: *letto.*

Mettere = to put

Preterit: *misi, mettesti, mise, mettemmo, metteste, misero.*

Past part.: *messo.*

Morire = to die

Ind. pres.: *muoio, muori, muore, moriamo, morite, muoiono.*

Future: *morirò* or *morrò, mor(i)rai, mor(i)rà, mor(i)remo, mor(i)rete, mor(i)ranno.*
Subj. pres.: *muoia, muoia, muoia, moriamo, moriate, muoiano.*
Cond. pres.: *morirei* or *morrei, mor(i)resti, mor(i)rebbe, mor(i)remmo, mor(i)reste, mor(i)rebbero.*
Pres. part.: *morente.*
Past part.: *morto.*

Nascere = to be born
Preterit: *nacqui, nascesti, nacque, nascemmo, nasceste, nacquero.*
Past part.: *nato.*

Nuocere = to hurt, to harm
Ind. pres.: *nuoco, nuoci, nuoce, nociamo, nocete, nuocono.*
Preterit: *nocqui, nocesti, nocque, nocemmo, noceste, nocquero.*
Subj. pres.: *noccia, noccia, noccia, nocciamo, nocciate, nocciano.*
Past part.: *nociuto.*

Piacere = to please, to like
Ind. pres.: *piaccio, piaci, piace, piacciamo, piacete, piacciono.*
Preterit: *piacqui, piacesti, piacque, piacemmo, piaceste, piacquero.*
Subj. pres.: *piaccia, piaccia, piaccia, piac(c)iamo, piac(c)iato, piacessero.*
Past part.: *piaciuto.*

Piovere = to rain
Preterit: *piovve, piovvero.*
Past part.: *piovuto.*

Potere = to be able
Ind. pres.: *posso, puoi, può, possiamo, potete, possono.*
Future: *potrò, potrai, potrà, potremo, potrete, potranno.*
Subj. pres.: *possa, possa, possa, possiamo, possiate, possano.*

Cond. pres.: *potrei, portresti, potrebbe, potremmo, potreste, potrebbero.*

Ridere = to laugh
Preterit: *risi, ridesti, rise, ridemmo, rideste, risero.*
Past part.: *riso.*

Rimanere = to stay
Ind. pres.: *rimango, rimani, rimane, rimaniamo, rimanete, rimangono.*
Preterit: *rimasi, rimanesti, rimase, rimanemmo, rimaneste, rimasero.*
Future: *rimarrò, rimarrai, rimarrà, rimarremo, rimarrete, rimarranno.*
Subj. pres.: *rimanga, rimanga, rimanga, rimaniamo, rimaniate, rimangano.*
Cond. pres.: *rimarrei, rimarresti, rimarrebbe, rimarremmo, rimarreste, rimarrebbero.*
Past part.: *rimasto.*

Rispondere = to answer
Preterit: *risposi, rispondesti, rispose, rispondemmo, rispondeste, risposero.*
Past part.: *risposto.*

Salire = to go up, to climb
Ind. pres.: *salgo, sali, sale, saliamo, salite, salgono.*
Subj. pres.: *salga, salga, salga, saliamo, saliate, salgano.*
Imperative: *sali, salga, saliamo, salite, salgano.*
Past part.: *salito.*

Sapere = to know
Ind. pres.: *so, sai, sa, sappiamo, sapete, sanno.*
Future: *saprò, saprai, saprà, sapremo, saprete, sapranno.*
Preterit: *seppi, sapesti, seppe, sapemmo, sapeste, seppero.*
Subj. pres.: *sappia, sappia, sappia, sappiamo, sappiate, sappiano.*
Imperative: *sappi, sappia, sappiamo, sappiate, sappiano.*

Cond. pres.: *saprei, sapresti, saprebbe, sapremmo, sapreste, saprebbero.*
Past part.: *saputo.*

Scegliere = to choose, select
Ind. pres.: *scelgo, scegli, sceglie, scegliamo, scegliete, scelgono.*
Preterit: *scelsi, scegliesti, scelse, scegliemmo, sceglieste, scelsero.*
Subj. pres.: *scelga, scelga, scelga, scegliamo, scegliate, scelgano.*
Imperative: *scegli, scelga, scegliamo, scegliete, scelgano.*
Past part.: *scelto.*

Scendere = to go down, descend
Preterit: *scesi, scendeste, scese, scendemmo, scendeste, scesero.*
Past part.: *sceso.*

Scrivere = to write
Preterit: *scrissi, scrivesti, scrisse, scrivemmo, scriveste, scrissero.*
Past part.: *scritto.*

Sedere = to sit
Ind. pres.: *siedo* or *seggo, siedi, siede, sediamo, sedete, siedono* or *seggono.*
Subj. pres.: *sieda* or *segga, sieda/segga, sieda/segga, sediamo, sediate, siedano (seggano).*
Imperative: *siedi, sieda* or *segga, sediamo, sedete, siedano (seggano).*

Stare = to stay; to remain (to be)
Ind. pres.: *sto, stai, sta, stiamo, state, stanno.*
Preterit: *stetti, stesti, stette, stemmo, steste, stettero.*
Future: *starò, starai, starà, staremo, starete, staranno.*
Subj. pres.: *stia, stia, stia, stiamo, stiate, stiano.*
Subj. imper.: *stessi, stessi, stesse, stessimo, steste, stessero.*

Imperative: *sta'*, *stia*, *stiamo*, *stiate*, *stiano*.
Cond. pres.: *starei*, *staresti*, *starebbe*, *staremmo*, *stareste*, *starebbero*.
Past part.: *stato*.

Tacere = to be silent
Ind. pres.: *taccio*, *taci*, *tace*, *taciamo*, *tacete*, *tacciono*.
Preterit: *tacqui*, *tacesti*, *tacque*, *tacemmo*, *taceste*, *tacquero*.
Subj. pres.: *taccia*, *taccia*, *taccia*, *taciamo*, *taciate*, *tacciano*.
Imperative: *taci*, *taccia*, *tacciamo*, *tacete*, *tacciano*.
Past part.: *taciuto*.

Udire = to hear, listen
Ind. pres.: *odo*, *odi*, *ode*, *udiamo*, *udite*, *odono*.
Future: *udrò*, *udrai*, *udrà*, *udremo*, *udrete*, *udranno*.
Subj. pres.: *oda*, *oda*, *oda*, *udiamo*, *udiate*, *odano*.
Condit.: *udirei*, *udresti*, *udrebbe*, *udremmo*, *udreste*, *udrebbero*.
Imperative: *odi*, *oda*, *udiamo*, *udite*, *odano*.

Uscire = to go out
Ind. pres.: *esco*, *esci*, *esce*, *usciamo*, *uscite*, *escono*.
Subj. pres.: *esca*, *esca*, *esca*, *usciamo*, *usciate*, *escano*.
Imperative: *esci*, *esca*, *usciamo*, *uscite*, *escano*.

Vedere = to see
Ind. pres.: *vedo*, *vedi*, *vede*, *vediamo*, *vedete*, *vedono*.
Preterit: *vidi*, *videsti*, *vide*, *videmmo*, *videste*, *videro*.
Future: *vedro*, *vedrai*, *vedrà*, *vedremo*, *vedrete*, *vedranno*.
Past part.: *veduto* or *visto*.

Venire = to come
Ind. pres.: *vengo*, *vieni*, *viene*, *veniamo*, *venite*, *vengono*.
Preterit: *venni*, *venisti*, *venne*, *venimmo*, *veniste*, *vennero*.
Future: *verrò*, *verrai*, *verrà*, *verremo*, *verrete*, *verranno*.
Subj. pres.: *venga*, *venga*, *venga*, *veniamo*, *veniate*, *vengano*.
Imperative: *vieni*, *venga*, *veniamo*, *venite*, *vengano*.
Cond. pres.: *verrei*, *verresti*, *verrebbe*, *verremmo*, *verreste*, *verrebbero*.

Pres. part.: *veniente*.
Past part.: *venuto*.

Vivere = to live
Preterit: *vissi, vivesti, visse, vivemmo, viveste, vissero*.
Future: *vivrò, vivrai, vivrà, vivremo, vivrete, vivranno*.
Cond. pres.: *vivrei, vivresti, vivrebbe, vivremmo, vivreste, vivrebbero*.
Past part.: *vissuto*.

Volere = to want
Ind. pres.: *voglio, vuoi, vuole, vogliamo, volete, vogliono*.
Preterit: *volli, volesti, volle, volemmo, voleste, vollero*.
Future: *vorrò, vorrai, vorrà, vorremo, vorrete, vorranno*.
Subj. pres.: *voglia, voglia, voglia, vogliamo, vogliate, vogliano*.
Cond. pres.: *vorrei, vorresti, vorrebbe, vorremmo, vorreste, vorrebbero*.
Past part.: *voluto*.

LETTER WRITING

A. FORMAL INVITATIONS AND ACCEPTANCES
INVITI FORMALI

marzo 2002

Il signore e la signora Peretti hanno il piacere di annunciare il matrimonio della loro figlia Maria con il signor Giovanni Rossi, ed hanno l'onore di invitare la Signoria Vostra alla cerimonia che avrà luogo nella Chiesa di San Giuseppe, il sei di questo mese, alle ore dodici. Dopo la cerimonia un ricevimento sarà dato in onore degli sposi nella casa dei genitori della sposa.

March 2002

Mr. and Mrs. Peretti take pleasure in announcing the wedding of their daughter Maria to Mr. Giovanni Rossi, and have the honor of inviting you to the ceremony, which will take place at the Church of San Giuseppe on the sixth of this month at twelve noon. There will be a reception for the newlyweds afterward at the residence of the bride's parents.

---

settembre 2002

Il signore e la signora De Marchi hanno il piacere di invitare il signor Rossi e la sua gentile signora a cena lunedì prossimo, alle otto.

September 2002

Mr. and Mrs. De Marchi take pleasure in inviting Mr. and Mrs. Rossi to dinner next Monday at eight o'clock.

---

marzo 2002

Il signore e la signora Martini hanno il piacere di invitare il signore e la signora Parisi al ricevimento in onore della loro figlia Anna, domenica sera, 19 marzo, alle ore nove.

March 2002

Mr. and Mrs. Martini take pleasure in inviting Mr. and Mrs. Parisi to a party in honor of their daughter Anna, on Sunday evening, March 19, at nine o'clock.

RESPONSES
RISPOSTE

Il signor Parisi e signora ringraziano per il cortese invito, felici di prendere parte al ricevimento del 19 marzo p.v.

Thank you for your kind invitation. We will be honored to attend the reception on March 19th.

[Note: *p.v.* = *prossimo venturo*, which means "the next coming" (month). *c.m.* = *corrente mese*, which means "of this month" (the running month.)]

I coniugi Rossi accettano il gentile invito per lunedì prossimo e ringraziano sentitamente.

Mr. and Mrs. Rossi will be honored to have dinner with Mr. and Mrs. De Marchi next Monday. With kindest regards.

I coniugi Rossi ringraziano sentitamente il signore e la signora Peretti per il cortese invito, spiacenti che impegni precedenti non permettano loro di poter accettare.

Mr. and Mrs. Rossi thank Mr. and Mrs. Peretti for their kind invitation and regret that they are unable to come due to a previous engagement.

B.   THANK-YOU NOTES
Biglietti Di Ringraziamento

Roma, 5 marzo 2002

Cara Anna,

Poche righe soltanto per sapere come stai e per ringraziarti del bellissimo vaso che mi hai regalato. L'ho messo sul pianoforte, e ti assicuro che è bellissimo.

Spero di vederti il mese prossimo al ricevimento di Angela. Sono sicura che la festa sarà molto divertente.

Mi auguro che la tua famiglia stia bene, come posso assicuràrti della mia. Ti saluto affettuosamente.

Maria

March 5, 2002

Dear Anna,

Just a few lines to say hello and also to let you know that I received the beautiful vase you sent me as a gift. I've put it on the piano, and you can't imagine how nice it looks.

I hope to see you at Angela's party next month. I think it's going to be a lot of fun.

I hope your family is all well. Everyone here is fine.

Affectionately,

Maria

C. BUSINESS LETTERS
LETTERE COMMERCIALI

Cavatorta & Co.,
Via Veneto 125,
Roma—Italia

Ditta Marini e Figli
Via Nomentana 11,
Roma.

Roma, 2 aprile, 2002

Gentili Signori:

   Abbiamo il piacere di presentarvi il portatore di questa lettera, signor Carlo Fontanesi, che è uno dei nostri agenti attualmente in vista alle principali città del vostro paese. Inutile aggiungere che qualsiasi gentilezza sarà usata al signor Fontanesi sarà da noi gradita come un personale favore.

   Ringraziandovi in anticipo, vi inviamo i nostri distinti saluti.

Cavatorta & Co.
il Presidente

Cavatorta & Co.
125 Veneto Street
Rome—Italy

(Firm) Marini & Sons
11 Nomentana Street
Rome

April 2, 2002

Gentlemen:

We have the pleasure of introducing to you the bearer of this letter, Mr. Carlo Fontanesi, one of our salesmen, who is visiting the principal cities of your country. Needless to add, we shall greatly appreciate any courtesy you extend to him. (It is needless to say to you that we shall consider any courtesy you extend to him as a personal favor.)

Thanking you in advance, we send our best regards.

Cavatorta & Co.
President

Milano, 3 marzo 2002
Signor Giulio Perri
direttore de "Il Mondo"
Via Montenapoleone 3,
Milano.

Gentile Signore:

   Includo un assegno di ¶100 (cento) per un anno di abbonamento alla sua rivista.

Distintamente

Lucia Landi

Lucia Landi
Corso Vittorio Emanuele, 8
Roma.

March 3, 2002

Mr. Giulio Perri
Editor of *The World*
3 Montenapoleone Street
Milan

Dear Sir:
   Enclosed please find a check for 100 euros for a year's subscription to your magazine.

Very truly yours,
Lucia Landi

Lucia Landi
8 Corso Vittorio Emanuele
Rome

D. Informal Letters
Lettere Informale

Caro Giuseppe,

  Sono stato molto lieto di ricevere la tua ultima lettera. Prima di tutto desidero darti la grande notizia. Ho finalmente deciso di fare un viaggio fino a Roma, dove intendo rimanere tutto il mese di maggio. Anna verrà con me. Lei è molto felice che avrà così l'occasione di conoscere voi due. Cerca, perciò, di essere possibilmente libero, per allora.

  Gli affari vanno bene, e spero che il buon vento continui. L'altro giorno ho visto Antonio, e lui mi ha chiesto tue notizie.

  Ti sarei grato se vorrai riservarci una camera all'albergo Nazionale. Scrivi presto. Saluti ad Elena.

tuo
Giovanni

Dear Giuseppe,

I was very happy to get your last letter. First of all, let me give you the big news. I have finally decided to make a trip to Rome, where I expect to spend all of May. Anna will come with me. She is extremely happy to be able to meet the two of you at last. Try therefore to be as free as you can then.

Business is good now, and I hope will keep that way (that the good wind will continue). I saw Antonio the other day and he asked me about you.

I'd be grateful to you if you would try to reserve a room for us at the National Hotel. Write soon. Give my regards to Helen.

Yours,
Giovanni

E. FORMS OF SALUTATIONS

Formal

Signore	Sir
Signora	Madam (Mrs.)
Signorina	Miss
Signor Professore	My dear Professor
Gentile Signor Rossi	My dear Mr. Rossi
Gentile Signora Rossi	My dear Mrs. Rossi
Gentile Signorina Rossi	My dear Miss Rossi

Informal

Caro Antonio	My dear Antonio
Cara Anna	My dear Anna
Mia amata	My beloved (f.)
Mio amato	My beloved (m.)
Carissimo Paolo	Dearest Paolo
Carissima Giovanna	Dearest Giovanna

F. FORMS OF COMPLIMENTARY CLOSINGS

Formal

1. *Gradisca i miei piu distinti saluti* (The *Lei* form is used.)

   Very truly yours. (Accept my most distinguished greetings.)

2. *Gradite i miei distinti saluti*. (The *voi* form is used.)

   Very truly yours. (Accept my distinguished greetings.)

3. *Voglia gradire i miei sinceri saluti*. (The *Lei* form is used.)

   Yours truly. (Accept my sincere greetings.)

4. *Vogliate gradire miei cordiali saluti* (The *voi* form is used.)

Yours truly. (Accept my heartfelt greetings.)

5. *Devotissimi.* (Can be shortened to *Dev. mo.)* (The plural form is used.)

Yours truly. (Your very devoted.)

6. *Devotissimo* (Shortened to *Dev. mo.)* (The singular form is used.)

Yours truly. (Your very devoted.)

Informal

1. *Ricevete i nostri saluti.*

Very sincerely. (Receive our heartfelt greetings.)

2. *In attesa di vostre notizie vi invio i miei sinceri e cordiali saluti.*

Sincerely yours (Waiting for your news, I send you my sincere and heartfelt greetings.)

3. *Sperando di ricevere presto tue notizie ti invio cordialissimi saluti.*

Sincerely yours. (Waiting to hear from you soon, I send you my most heartfelt greetings.)

4. *Tuo amico.*

Sincerely. (Your friend, m.)

5. *Tua amica.*

Sincerely. (Your friend, f.)

6. *Affettuosissimo.* (Shortened to *Aff. mo)*

Affectionately yours. (Very affectionate, m.)

7. *Affettuosissima.* (Shortened to *Aff. ma)*

Affectionately yours (Very affectionate, f.)

8. *Affezionatissimo/a (Aff. mo)*	Affectionately yours. (Very affectionate.)
9. *Le invio cordiali saluti.*	Sincerely. (I send you heartfelt greetings.) *(polite)*
10. *Ti invio cordiali saluti e abbracci.*	Sincerely. (I send you heartfelt greetings and embraces.) *(familiar)*
11. *Con mille abbracci e baci.*	Love. (With a thousand embraces and kisses.)
12. *Abbracciandoti e baciandoti caramente.*	Love. (Embracing and kissing you dearly.)
13. *Un abbraccio,*	Love, (Hugs,)

G. FORMS OF THE ENVELOPE

Signor
Paolo Bolla
Via Veneto 10
Roma

> Angelo Rossi
> Piazza Roma
> Napoli

Via Nomentana 27
Roma

> Marcello Marini
> Via Montenapoleone
> Milano

Signorina Anna Rossi
Piazza Vittorio
Emanuele 9
Firenze

> Silvana Tarri
> Piazza Venezia 71
> Roma